QUICK & EASY, PROVEN RECIPES
Vegetarian

D1390246

Publisher's Note: Raw or semi-cooked eggs should not be consumed by babies, toddlers, pregnant or breastfeeding women, the elderly or those suffering from a chronic illness.

Publisher & Creative Director: Nick Wells
Project Editor: Catherine Taylor
Art Director: Mike Spender
Layout Design: Jane Ashley
Digital Design & Production: Chris Herbert

Special thanks to Esme Chapman, Laura Bulbeck and Frances Bodiam.

FLAME TREE PUBLISHING
6 Melbray Mews, Fulham,
London SW6 3NS
United Kingdom
www.flametreepublishing.com

This edition first published 2018

ISBN: 978-1-78755-097-1

QUICK & EASY, PROVEN RECIPES

Vegetarian

General Editor: Gina Steer

**FLAME TREE
PUBLISHING**

Contents

Nutrition
& Basic
Ingredients

Before you get stuck into the wealth of delicious vegetarian recipes this book has to offer, take a moment to brush up on your ingredient basics. Covering rice, pasta, potatoes, vegetables and salad, this section gives you the low-down on the different varieties available, as well as nutritional information, preparation guidelines and cooking advice for techniques ranging from microwaving and steaming to roasting and grilling.

Nutrition

ℰ

Home-cooked meals are a great way to provide us with a healthy and well-balanced diet, the body's primary energy source. In children, a healthy diet is the basis of future health and provides lots of energy. In adults, it encourages self-healing and regeneration within the body. A well-balanced, varied diet will provide the body with all the essential nutrients it needs. The ideal variety of foods is shown in the pyramid below.

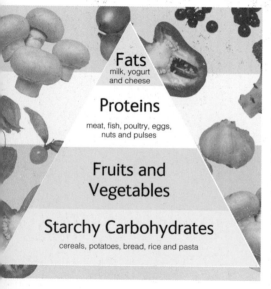

Fats
milk, yogurt
and cheese

Proteins
meat, fish, poultry, eggs,
nuts and pulses

**Fruits and
Vegetables**

Starchy Carbohydrates
cereals, potatoes, bread, rice and pasta

Fats

Fats fall into two categories: saturated and unsaturated fats. It is very important that a healthy balance is achieved within the diet. Fats are an essential part of the diet and a source of energy and provide essential fatty acids and fat–soluble vitamins. The right balance of fats should boost the body's immunity to infection and keep muscles, nerves and arteries in good condition. Saturated fats are of animal origin and are hard when stored at room temperature. They can be found in dairy produce, eggs, margarines as well as in manufactured products such as pies, biscuits and cakes. A high intake of saturated fat over many years has been proven to increase heart disease and high blood cholesterol levels and often leads to weight gain. The aim of a healthy diet is to keep the fat content low in the foods that we eat. Lowering the amount of saturated fat that we consume is very important, but this does not mean that it is good to consume lots of other types of fat.

There are two kinds of unsaturated fats: polyunsaturated fats and monounsaturated fats. Polyunsaturated fats include the following oils: safflower oil, soybean oil, corn oil and sesame oil. Within the polyunsaturated group are Omega oils. The Omega-3 oils are of significant interest because they have been found to be particularly beneficial to coronary health and can encourage brain growth and development. Omega-3 oils are derived from oily fish. However, for vegetarians, good sources of the alpha-linolenic-acid type of Omega 3 (ALA) include linseeds/flaxseeds, chia seeds, hemp seeds, walnuts and purslane. Additionally, vegetarian supplements made from microalgae are available in most supermarkets and health shops. The most popular oils that are high in monounsaturates are olive oil, sunflower oil and peanut oil. The Mediterranean diet, which is based on foods high in monounsaturated fats, is recommended for heart health. Also, monounsaturated fats are known to help reduce the levels of LDL (the bad) cholesterol.

Proteins

Composed of amino acids (proteins' building bricks), proteins perform a wide variety of functions for the body, including supplying energy and building and repairing tissue. Good sources of proteins are eggs, milk, yogurt, nuts and pulses. (See the second level of the pyramid.) Some of these foods, however, contain saturated fats. For a nutritional balance, eat generous amounts of soya beans, lentils, peas and nuts.

Fruits and Vegetables

Not only are fruits and vegetables the most visually appealing foods, but they are extremely good for us, providing vital vitamins and minerals essential for growth, repair and protection in the human body. Fruits and vegetables are low in calories and are responsible for regulating the body's metabolic processes and controlling the composition of its fluids and cells.

Minerals

∾ Calcium – Important for healthy bones and teeth, nerve transmission, muscle contraction, blood clotting and hormone function. Calcium promotes a healthy heart, improves skin, relieves aching muscles and bones, maintains the correct acid-alkaline balance and reduces menstrual cramps. Good sources are dairy products, nuts, pulses, fortified white flours, breads and green, leafy vegetables.

∾ Chromium – Part of the glucose tolerance factor, chromium balances blood sugar levels, helps to normalise hunger and reduce cravings, improves lifespan, helps protect DNA and is essential for heart function. Good sources are brewer's yeast, wholemeal bread, rye bread, potatoes, green peppers, butter and parsnips.

∾ Iodine – Important for thyroid hormones and for normal development. Good sources of iodine are seaweed, milk and dairy products.

∾ Iron – As a component of haemoglobin, iron carries oxygen around the body. It is vital for normal growth and development. Good sources are fortified breakfast cereals, pulses, green, leafy vegetables, egg yolk and cocoa and cocoa products.

∾ Magnesium – Important for efficient functioning of metabolic enzymes and development of the skeleton. Magnesium promotes healthy muscles by helping them to relax and is therefore good for PMS. It is also important for heart muscles and the nervous system. Good sources are nuts, green vegetables, cereals, milk and yogurt.

Phosphorus – Forms and maintains bones and teeth, builds muscle tissue, helps maintain the body's pH and aids metabolism and energy production. Phosphorus is present in almost all foods.

 Potassium – Enables nutrients to move into cells, while waste products move out; promotes healthy nerves and muscles; maintains fluid balance in the body; helps secretion of insulin for blood sugar control to produce constant energy; relaxes muscles; maintains heart functioning and stimulates gut movement to encourage proper elimination. Good sources are fruit, vegetables, milk and bread.

 Selenium – Antioxidant properties help to protect against free radicals and carcinogens. Selenium reduces inflammation, stimulates the immune system to fight infections, promotes a healthy heart and helps vitamin E's action. It is also required for the male reproductive system and is needed for metabolism. Good sources are eggs, cereals, nuts and dairy products.

 Sodium – Helps to control body fluid and balance, preventing dehydration. Sodium is involved in muscle and nerve function and helps move nutrients into cells. All foods are good sources, but pickled and salted foods are richest in sodium.

 Zinc – Important for metabolism and the healing of wounds. It also aids ability to cope with stress, promotes a healthy nervous system and brain, especially in the growing foetus, aids bone and tooth formation and is essential for constant energy. Good sources are pulses, wholegrain cereals and nuts.

Nutrition

Vitamins

- Vitamin A – Important for cell growth and development and for the formation of visual pigments in the eye. Found in whole milk, red and yellow fruits and carrots.

- Vitamin B1 – Important in releasing energy from carbohydrate-containing foods. Good sources are yeast and yeast products, bread, fortified breakfast cereals and potatoes.

- Vitamin B2 – Important for metabolism of proteins, fats and carbohydrates. Found in yeast extract, fortified cereals and milk.

- Vitamin B3 – Helps the metabolism of food into energy. Sources are milk and milk products, fortified breakfast cereals, pulses and eggs.

- Vitamin B5 – Important for the metabolism of food and energy production. All foods are good sources, but especially fortified breakfast cereals, wholegrain bread and dairy products.

- Vitamin B6 – Important for metabolism of protein and fat. Vitamin B6 may also be involved with the regulation of sex hormones. Good sources are soya beans and peanuts.

- Vitamin B12 – Important for the production of red blood cells and DNA. It is vital for growth and the nervous system. Good sources are eggs and milk.

- Biotin – Important for metabolism of fatty acids. Good sources of biotin are eggs and nuts. Micro-organisms also manufacture this vitamin in the gut.

- Vitamin C – Important for healing wounds and the formation of collagen, which keeps skin and bones strong. It is an important antioxidant. Sources are fruits and vegetables.

- Vitamin D – Important for absorption of calcium to build bone strength. Sources are eggs, whole milk and milk products, margarine and sunlight – vitamin D is made in the skin.

- Vitamin E – Important as an antioxidant vitamin, helping to protect cell membranes from damage. Good sources are vegetable oils, margarines, seeds, nuts and green vegetables.

- Folic Acid – Critical during pregnancy for the development of foetus brain and nerves. It is essential for brain and nerve function and is needed for protein and red blood cell formation. Sources are wholegrain cereals, fortified cereals, green, leafy vegetables and oranges.

- Vitamin K – Important for controlling blood clotting. Sources are cauliflower, Brussels sprouts, lettuce, cabbage, beans, broccoli, peas, asparagus, potatoes, corn oil, tomatoes and milk.

Carbohydrates

Carbohydrates come in two basic forms: starchy and sugar carbohydrates. Starchy carbohydrates, also known as complex carbohydrates, include cereals, potatoes, breads, rice and pasta. (See the fourth level of the pyramid). Eating wholegrain varieties also provides fibre, beneficial in preventing bowel cancer, and controlling cholesterol weight. Sugar carbohydrates, known as fast-release carbohydrates (because of the quick fix of energy they give), include sugar and sugar-sweetened products such as jams and syrups. Milk provides lactose, which is milk sugar, and fruits provide fructose, which is fruit sugar.

Nutrition

Rice

Rice is the staple food of many countries throughout the world. Every country and culture has its own repertoire of rice recipes – India, for example, has the aromatic biryani, Spain has the saffron-scented paella, and Italy has the creamy risotto. Rice is grown on marshy, flooded land where other cereals cannot thrive, and because it is grown in so many different areas, there is a huge range of rice types.

Varieties

∾ **Long-grain white rice** – Probably the most widely used type of rice. Long-grain white rice has been milled so that the husk, bran and germ are removed. Easy-cook long-grain white rice has been steamed under pressure before milling. Precooked rice, also known as parboiled or converted rice, is polished white rice that is half-cooked after milling, then dried again. It is quick to cook, but has a bland flavour.

∾ **Long-grain brown rice** – Where the outer husk is removed, leaving the bran and germ behind. This retains more of the fibre, vitamins and minerals. It has a nutty flavour and slightly chewy texture and takes longer to cook than white rice.

∾ **Basmati rice** – This slender, long-grain rice, which may be white or brown, is grown in the foothills of the Himalayas. After harvesting, it is allowed to mature for a year, giving it a unique aromatic flavour, hence its name, which means fragrant.

- **Risotto rice** – Grown in the north of Italy, this is the only rice that is suitable for making risotto. The grains are plump and stubby and have the ability to absorb large quantities of liquid without becoming too soft, cooking to a creamy texture with a slight bite. There are two grades of risotto rice: superfino and fino. Arborio rice is the most widely sold variety of the former, but you may also find carnaroli, Roma and baldo in Italian delicatessens. Fino rice such as vialone nano has a slightly shorter grain, but the flavour is still excellent.

- **Valencia rice** – Traditionally used for Spanish paella, Valencia rice is soft and tender when ready. The medium-sized grains break down easily, so should be left unstirred during cooking to absorb the flavour of the stock and other ingredients.

- **Jasmine rice** – Also known as Thai fragrant rice, this long-grain rice has a delicate, almost perfumed aroma and flavour and has a soft, sticky texture.

- **Japanese sushi rice** – This is a fairly glutinous rice in that it has a sticky texture. When mixed with rice vinegar, it is easy to roll up with a filling inside to make sushi.

- **Pudding rice** – This rounded, short-grain rice is ideal for rice desserts. The grains swell and absorb large quantities of milk during cooking, giving puddings a rich, creamy consistency.

- **Wild rice** – This is an aquatic grass grown in North America rather than a true variety of rice. The black grains are long and slender and, after harvesting and cleaning, they are toasted to remove the chaff and intensify the nutty flavour and slight chewiness. It is often sold as a mixture with long-grain rice.

- **Rice flour** – Raw rice can be finely ground to make rice flour, which may be used to thicken sauces (1 tbsp will thicken 300 ml/ 1/2 pint) or in Asian desserts. It is also used to make rice noodles.

Rice

Health and Nutrition

Rice is low in fat and high in complex carbohydrates, which are absorbed slowly and help to maintain blood sugar levels. It is also a reasonable source of protein and provides many B vitamins and the minerals potassium and phosphorus. It is a gluten-free cereal, making it suitable for coeliacs. Brown rice is richer in nutrients and fibre than refined white rice.

Buying and Storing Rice

Rice will keep for several years if kept in sealed packets. However, it is at its best when fresh. To ensure freshness, always buy rice from reputable shops with a good turnover and buy in small quantities.

Once opened, store the rice in an airtight container in a cool, dry place to keep out moisture. Most rice (but not risotto) benefits from washing before cooking – tip into a sieve and rinse under cold running water until the water runs clear. This removes any starch still clinging to the grains.

Cooked rice will keep for up to 2 days if cooled and stored in a covered bowl in the refrigerator. If eating rice cold, serve within 24 hours – after this time, it should be thoroughly reheated.

How to Cook Rice

There are countless ways to cook rice, but much depends on the variety of rice being used, the dish being prepared and the desired results. Each variety of rice has its own characteristics. Some types of rice cook to light, separate grains, some to a rich, creamy consistency and some to a consistency where the grains stick together. Different types of rice have different powers of absorption. Long-grain rice will absorb three times its weight in water, whereas 25 g/1 oz short-grain pudding rice can soak up a massive 300 ml/¹/₂ pint liquid.

Cooking Long-grain Rice

The simplest method of cooking long-grain rice is to add it to plenty of boiling, salted water in a large saucepan. Allow 50 g/2 oz rice per person when cooking as an accompaniment.

1. Rinse under cold running water until clear, then tip into rapidly boiling water.

2. Stir once, then, when the water returns to the boil, reduce the heat and simmer uncovered.

3. Allow 10–12 minutes for white rice and 30–40 minutes for brown – check the packet for specific timings.

4. The easiest way to test if rice is cooked is to bite a couple of grains – they should be tender but still firm.

5. Drain immediately, then return to the pan with a little butter and herbs, if liked. Fluff up with a fork and serve.

To keep the rice warm, put it in a bowl and place over a pan of barely simmering water. Cover the top of the bowl with a tea towel until ready to serve.

Rice

Absorption Method

Cooking rice using the absorption method is also simple. This method is good for cooking jasmine and Valencia rice. Weigh out the quantity, then measure it by volume in a measuring jug – you will need 150 ml/¼ pint for two people.

1. Rinse the rice, then tip into a large saucepan. If liked, cook the rice in a little butter or oil for 1 minute.

2. Pour in 2 parts water or stock to 1 part rice, season with salt and bring to the boil.

3. Cover, then simmer gently until the liquid is absorbed and the rice is tender. White rice will take 15 minutes to cook, whereas brown rice will take 35 minutes. If there is still a little liquid left when the rice is tender, uncover and cook for 1 minute until evaporated.

4. Remove from the heat and leave covered for 4–5 minutes, then fluff up before serving.

Oven-baked Method

The oven-baked method works by absorption too, but takes longer than cooking on the hob. For oven-baked rice for two:

1. Fry a chopped onion in 1 tablespoon olive oil in a 1.2 litre/ 2 pint flameproof casserole dish until soft and golden.

2. Add 75 g/3 oz long-grain rice and cook for 1 minute.

3. Stir in 300 ml/¹/₂ pint stock – add a finely pared strip of lemon zest or a bay leaf, if liked.

4. Cover and bake in a preheated oven at 180°C/ 350°F/Gas Mark 4 for 40 minutes, or until the rice is tender and all the stock has been absorbed. Fluff up before serving.

Cooking in the Microwave

1. Place the rinsed long-grain rice in a large heatproof bowl.

2. Add boiling water or stock, allowing 300 ml/¹/₂ pint for 125 g/4 oz rice and 500 ml/18 fl oz for 225 g/8 oz rice. Add a pinch salt and a knob butter, if desired.

3. Cover with pierced clingfilm and cook on high for 3 minutes.

4. Stir, re-cover and cook on medium for 12 minutes for white rice and 25 minutes for brown.

5. Leave covered for 5 minutes before fluffing up and serving.

Cooking in a Pressure Cooker

Follow the quantities given for the absorption method and bring to the boil in the pressure cooker. Stir, cover and bring to a high 6.8 kg/15 lb pressure. Lower the heat and cook for 5 minutes if white rice or 8 minutes if brown.

Cooking in a Rice Cooker

Follow the quantities given for the absorption method. Put the rice, salt and boiling water or stock in the cooker, return to the boil and cover. When all the liquid has been absorbed, the cooker will turn off automatically.

Pasta

Pasta Varieties

There are two types of dried pasta: 'secca' is factory-made from wheat and water and 'pasta all'uovo' is made with eggs. Egg pasta can be bought 'fresh', but should be used within 3 days of opening, so dried tends to be a more useful store-cupboard ingredient.

- Buckwheat – A gluten-free pasta made from buckwheat flour.

- Coloured and flavoured pasta – Varieties are endless, the most popular being spinach and tomato. Others include beetroot, herb, garlic, chilli, mushroom and black ink.

- Durum wheat pasta – Most readily available and may be made with or without eggs. Look for 'durum wheat' or 'pasta di semola di grano duro' on the packet, as pastas made from soft wheat tend to become soggy when cooked.

- Wholemeal pasta – Made with wholemeal flour, this has a higher fibre content than ordinary pasta. Wholemeal pasta takes longer to cook than the refined version.

Pasta Shapes

There are numerous different shapes and some of the most popular ones are listed opposite.

Long Pasta

- **Spaghetti** – Probably the best-known type of pasta, spaghetti derives its name from the word 'spago' meaning string, which describes its round, thin shape perfectly.

- **Tagliatelle** – Most common type of ribbon noodle pasta. It is traditionally from Bologna, where it accompanies bolognese sauce (rather than spaghetti). Fettuccine is the Roman version of tagliatelle and is cut slightly thinner.

Short Pasta

- **Conchiglie** – Pasta shapes resembling conch shells. Sizes vary from tiny to large. They may be smooth or ridged ('conchiglie rigate').

- **Eliche and fusilli** – These are twisted into the shape of a screw.

- **Farfalle** – Bow or butterfly shaped, often with crinkled edges.

- **Macaroni** – Known as elbow macaroni or maccheroni in Italy. A thin, quick-cook variety is also available.

- **Penne** – Slightly larger than macaroni, the ends of these tubes are cut and pointed like quills.

- **Pipe** – Curved, hollow pasta and often sold ridged as 'pipe rigate'.

- **Rigatoni** – Substantial, chunky, tubular pasta, often used for baking.

- **Rtelle** – Thin, wheel-shaped pasta, often sold in packets of two or three colours.

Pasta

Stuffed Pasta

- ∾ **Tortellini** – The most common variety, consisting of tiny, stuffed pieces of pasta. Larger ones are called tortelloni.

- ∾ **Cappelletti, ravioli and agnalotti** – These are sometimes sold dried, but are more often available fresh.

How to Cook Perfect Pasta

As an approximate guide, allow 75–125 g/3–4 oz uncooked pasta per person. The amount will depend on whether the pasta is being served for a light or main meal and the type of sauce that it is being served with. Follow a few simple rules to ensure that your pasta is cooked to perfection every time:

1. Choose a large saucepan – there needs to be plenty of room for the pasta to move around so it does not stick together.

2. Cook the pasta in a large quantity of fast-boiling, well-salted water, ideally 4 litres/7 pints water and 1¹/₂–2 tablespoons salt for every 350–450 g/12 oz–1 lb pasta.

3. Tip in the pasta all at once, stir and cover. Return to a rolling boil, then remove the lid. Once it is boiling, lower the heat to medium-high and cook the pasta for the required time. It should be al dente, or tender but still firm to the bite.

4. Drain, reserving a little of the cooking water to stir into the drained pasta. This helps to thin the sauce, if necessary, and helps prevent the pasta sticking together as it cools.

Potatoes

The humble potato is generally taken for granted and the versatility and huge number of varieties of this delicious vegetable are often forgotten. Worldwide, there are thousands of different types of potatoes and for about two-thirds of the world, they are the staple food.

General Guidance

Nutritionally, potatoes are high in complex carbohydrates, providing sustained energy. They are also an excellent source of vitamins B and C and minerals such as iron and potassium. They contain almost no fat and are high in dietary fibre.

Types

Potatoes are classified according to how early in the season they are ready for harvesting and are named as follows: first early, second early and maincrop. The first earlies (such as the Maris Bard variety) are the first new potatoes on the market; they are very fresh and young and the skins can simply be rubbed off. The second earlies (such as Anya) are still new potatoes, but their skins will have begun to set. These potatoes will be difficult to scrape and are better cooked in their skins. Maincrop potatoes (such as Maris Piper, King Edward, Charlotte, Désirée) are available all year round and may have been stored for several months.

Potatoes

Choosing

When buying potatoes, always choose ones with smooth, firm skins. When purchasing new potatoes, check that they are really young and fresh by scraping the skin – it should peel away very easily. Only buy the quantity you need and use within a couple of days.

Check maincrop potatoes to make sure that they are firm and not sprouting or showing any signs of mould. Avoid buying and discard any potatoes with greenish patches or carefully cut them out. These parts of the potato are toxic and a sign that they have been stored in light.

Storing

Potatoes should be stored in a cool, dark place, but not in the refrigerator, as the dampness will make them sweat, causing mould to grow. If the potatoes come in plastic bags, take them out and store in a paper bag or on a vegetable rack. If you prefer to buy in bulk, keep the potatoes in a cold, dark, dry place such as a larder or garage, making sure that they do not freeze in cold weather.

Sweet potatoes should be stored in a cool, dry place, but, unlike ordinary potatoes, do not need to be kept in the dark.

Which Potato for Which Method?

Generally, new potato varieties have a firm and waxy texture and do not break up during cooking, so are ideal for boiling, steaming and salads. Maincrop potatoes, on the other hand, have a more floury texture and lend themselves to mashing and roasting – both types are suitable for chips. Individual potato varieties have their own characteristics. Some maincrop varieties are better for boiling than baking and vice versa, so choose the most appropriate type of potato for the dish being prepared (check the label or ask your retailer).

Whichever way you choose to serve potatoes, allow 175–225 g/6–8 oz per person (about 4–6 new potatoes or 1–2 medium potatoes). (One whole smallish potato – 4.5–6 cm/1³/₄ –2¹/₂ inches in diameter – weighs around 175 g/6 oz; one whole medium potato – 5.5–8 cm/2¹/₄–3¹/₄ inches – weighs around 210 g/7½ oz; and one whole large potato – 7.5–11 cm/3–4¹/₄ inches – weighs around 375 g/13 oz.)

Boiling

New Potatoes

Most of the new potatoes available nowadays are fairly clean – especially those sold in supermarkets – and simply need a light scrub before cooking in their skins.

1. If the potatoes are very dirty, use a small scrubbing brush or scourer to remove both the skins and dirt (or leave the skins on if they are second earlies, and peel when cooked, if liked).

2. Add them to a pan of cold, salted water and bring to the boil. Cover the pan with a lid and simmer for 12–15 minutes until tender. Very firm new potatoes can be simmered for 8 minutes, then left to stand in the hot water for a further 10 minutes until cooked through.

3. Add a couple of fresh herbs sprigs to the pan if you like – fresh mint is traditionally used to flavour potatoes.

4. Drain the potatoes thoroughly and, if you want to peel them now, hold the hot potatoes with a fork to make this easier. Serve hot, tossed in a little melted butter or, for a change, a tablespoon of pesto.

'Old' (Maincrop) Potatoes

1. Choose a maincrop potato suitable for boiling, then peel thinly and cut into even-sized pieces. Alternatively, you can cook the potatoes in their skins and peel them after cooking.

Potatoes

2. Add to a saucepan of cold, salted water and bring to the boil. Cover the pan with a lid and simmer for 20 minutes, or until tender. Drain. (It is particularly important to cook floury potatoes gently or the outsides may start to fall apart before they are tender in the centre. Drain the potatoes in a colander, then return them to the pan to dry out over a very low heat for 1–2 minutes.)

Mashed Potatoes

1. Boil your maincrop potatoes as described and, once cooked, roughly mash and add a knob butter and 2 tablespoons milk per person. Mash until smooth, with a hand masher, grater or a potato ricer.

2. Season to taste with salt, freshly ground black pepper and a little freshly grated nutmeg, if liked, then beat for a few seconds with a wooden spoon until fluffy.

As an alternative to butter, use a good-quality olive oil or crème fraîche. Finely chopped red and green chillies, fresh herbs or grated vegetarian Italian hard cheese can also be stirred in for additional flavour.

Steaming Potatoes

All potatoes are suitable for steaming. Floury potatoes, however, are ideal for this method of cooking, as they fall apart easily when boiled.

1. New and small potatoes can be steamed whole, but larger ones should be cut into even-sized pieces.

2. Place the potatoes in a steamer, colander or sieve over boiling water and cover. Steam for 10 minutes if the potatoes are very small, or, if they are cut into large chunks, cook for 20–25 minutes.

Frying Potatoes

Chipped Potatoes

Slightly finer chips are known as pommes frites (or 'French fries'), even finer ones as pommes allumettes and the finest of all as pommes pailles (straw potatoes). Paper-thin slices of peeled potatoes, cut with a sharp knife or using a mandoline or food processor, can be deep-fried a few at a time to make crisps or game chips. To make standard chipped potatoes, however, proceed as follows:

1. Wash, peel and cut the potatoes into 1.5 cm/⅝ inch slices.

2. Place the strips in a bowl of cold water and leave for 20 minutes, then drain and dry well on paper towels – moisture will make the fat spit.

3. Pour some oil into a deep, heavy-based saucepan or deep-fat fryer, making sure that the oil does not go any further than halfway up the sides of the pan. Heat the oil to 190°C/375°F, or until a chip dropped into the fat rises to the surface straight away and is surrounded by bubbles.

4. Put the chips into a wire basket, lower into the oil and cook for 7–8 minutes until golden.

5. Remove and increase the heat of the oil to 200°C/400°F. Lower the chips into the oil again and cook for 2–3 minutes until they are crisp and golden brown. Drain excess oil on paper towels before serving.

Healthy Chips

To make lower-fat chips, preheat the oven to 200°C/400°F/Gas Mark 6 and place a nonstick baking tray in the oven to heat up.

Potatoes

1. Cut the potatoes into chips as above or into chunky wedges, if preferred. Put the chips or wedges in a pan of cold water and quickly bring to the boil.

2. Simmer for 2 minutes, then drain in a colander. Leave for a few minutes to dry.

3. Drizzle over 1 1/2–2 tablespoons olive or sunflower oil and toss to coat.

4. Tip onto the heated baking tray and cook in the preheated oven for 20–25 minutes, turning occasionally, until golden brown and crisp.

Sautéed Potatoes

1. Cut peeled potatoes into rounds about 0.5 cm/1/4 inch thick and pat dry.

2. Heat 25 g/1 oz/2 tbsp unsalted butter and 2 tablespoons oil in a large, heavy-based frying pan until hot.

3. Add the potatoes in a single layer and cook for 4–5 minutes until the undersides are golden. Turn with a large fish slice or spatula and cook the other side until golden and tender.

4. Drain on paper towels and sprinkle with a little salt before serving.

Baking Potatoes

Allow a large (300–375 g/11–13 oz) potato per person and choose a variety such as Maris Piper, Cara, King Edward, Russet Burbank or Russet Arcadia.

1. Wash and dry the potatoes, prick the skins lightly, then rub each one with a little oil and sprinkle with salt.

2. Bake at 200°C/400°F/Gas Mark 6 for 1–1¹/₂ hours until the skins are crisp and the centres are very soft. To speed up the cooking time, thread onto metal skewers, as this conducts heat to the middle of the potatoes.

Roasting Potatoes

For crisp and brown outsides and fluffy centres, choose potatoes suitable for baking.

1. Thinly peel the potatoes and cut into even-sized pieces.

2. Drop into a pan of boiling, salted water and simmer for 5 minutes.

3. Turn off the heat and leave for a further 3–4 minutes.

4. Drain well and return the potatoes to the pan over a low heat for a minute to dry them and to roughen the edges.

5. Carefully transfer them to a roasting tin containing hot oil. Baste well, then bake at 220°C/425°F/ Gas Mark 7 for 20 minutes.

6. Turn them and cook for a further 20–30 minutes, turning and basting at least one more time. Serve as soon as the potatoes are ready.

Potato Croquettes

1. Mash dry, boiled potatoes with just a little butter or olive oil.

2. Stir in 1 egg yolk mixed with 1–2 tablespoons milk or crème fraîche to make a firm mixture.

3. Shape the mashed potatoes into small cylinders about 5 cm/2 inches long and roll them in flour. Dip in beaten egg and then in fresh white breadcrumbs, then chill the croquettes in the refrigerator for 30 minutes.

4. Place a little unsalted butter and oil in a heavy-based frying pan and slowly heat until the butter has melted.

5. Shallow-fry the croquettes, turning occasionally, until they are golden brown and crisp.

Rosti

These small rostis can be elaborated on by adding other ingredients such as vegetables, herbs and spices, and making one big rosti.

1. Parboil peeled, waxy potatoes in boiling, salted water for 8 minutes, then drain and leave to cool.

2. Coarsely grate the potatoes into a bowl. Season well with salt and freshly ground black pepper and freshly chopped herbs, if liked.

3. Heat a mixture of unsalted butter and oil in a heavy-based frying pan until bubbling.

4. Add tablespoonfuls of the grated potato into the pan and flatten with the back of a fish slice. Cook over a medium heat for about 7 minutes until crisp and golden. Turn and cook the other side.

Cooking Potatoes in a Clay Pot

Terracotta potato pots can cook up to 450 g/1 lb whole potatoes (2–3 medium potatoes) at a time.

1. Soak the clay pot for at least 20 minutes before use, then add even-sized, preferably smallish, potatoes.

2. Drizzle over a little olive oil and season generously with salt and freshly ground black pepper.

3. Cover the pot with the lid and put in a cold oven, setting the temperature to 200°C/400°F/Gas Mark 6. The potatoes will take about 45 minutes to cook.

Microwaving Potatoes

The microwave can be used to boil new potatoes or peeled chunks of potato as follows:

1. To cook new potatoes in the microwave, prick the skins with a skewer to prevent them from bursting.

2. Place in a bowl with 3 tablespoons boiling water.

3. Cover with clingfilm which has been pierced two or three times and cook on high for 12–15 minutes until tender.

You can also 'bake' potatoes in the microwave, providing you do not want the skins to be crispy:

1. Place each potato on a circle of paper towels. Make several cuts in each to ensure that the skins do not burst.

2. Transfer to the microwave plate and cook on high for 4–6 minutes per potato, allowing an extra 3–4 minutes for every additional potato. Turn the potatoes at least once during cooking.

3. Leave to stand for 5 minutes before serving.

🥔 Potatoes

Vegetables & Salads

Vegetables add colour, texture, flavour and valuable nutrients to a meal. They play an important role in the diet, providing necessary vitamins, minerals and fibre. Vegetables are versatile: they can be served as an accompaniment to other dishes – they go well with pastas and starches – or they can be used as the basis for the whole meal.

Types of Vegetables

Vegetables are classified into different groups: leaf vegetables; roots and tubers; beans, pods and shoots; bulb vegetables; fruit vegetables; brassicas; cucumbers and squashes; sea vegetables; and mushrooms.

∾ **Leaf Vegetables** – This includes lettuce and other salad leaves, such as oakleaf, frisée, radicchio, lamb's lettuce and lollo rosso as well as rocket, spinach, Swiss chard and watercress. These are available all year round, as most are now grown under glass. Many leaf vegetables, such as watercress and spinach, are delicious cooked and made into soups.

∾ **Roots and Tubers** – This group includes beetroot, carrots, celeriac, daikon, Jerusalem artichokes, parsnips, potatoes, radishes, salsify, sweet potatoes, swede, turnips and yams. Most are available all year round.

- **Beans, Pods and Shoots** – This category includes all the beans, such as broad beans, French beans, mangetout and runner beans, as well as peas and sweetcorn, baby corn and okra. Shoots include asparagus, bamboo shoots, celery, chicory, fennel, globe artichokes and palm hearts. The majority are available all year round.

- **Bulb Vegetables** – This is the onion family and includes all the different types of onion, from the common brown-skinned globe onion, Italian red onion and Spanish onion to shallots, pickling onions, pearl onions and spring onions. This category also includes leeks, chives and garlic. All are available throughout the year.

- **Brassicas** – This is the cabbage family and includes all the different types of cabbage, broccoli, Brussels sprouts, cauliflower, curly kale, Chinese cabbage, pak choi and purple sprouting broccoli. Some of the cabbages are only seasonal, such as the winter cabbages Savoy cabbage and red cabbage, while there are also summer cabbages.

- **Fruit Vegetables** – This group originates from hot climates, such as the Mediterranean, and includes aubergines, avocados, chilli peppers, sweet peppers and tomatoes. These are available all year round, but are more plentiful in the summer.

- **Cucumbers and Squashes** – These vegetables are members of the gourd family and include cucumbers, gherkins, pumpkins and other squashes. There are two types of squash – summer squashes, which include courgettes, marrows and pattypan, and winter squashes, such as pumpkins and butternut, acorn, gem and spaghetti squashes. Courgettes and cucumbers are available all through the year, but pumpkins and other winter squashes and marrow are seasonal.

- **Sea Vegetables** – The vegetables from this group may be quite difficult to find in supermarkets. The most readily available are seaweed (normally available dried) and sea kale.

- **Mushrooms and Fungi** – This category includes all the different types of mushroom: the cultivated button mushrooms, chestnut mushrooms, large portobello or flat mushrooms, oyster and shiitake mushrooms, as well as wild mushrooms such as porcini (or ceps), morels, chanterelles and truffles. Cultivated mushrooms are available throughout the year, but wild ones are only around from late summer. If you collect your own wild mushrooms, make sure you correctly identify them before picking, as some are very poisonous and can be fatal if eaten. Dried mushrooms are also available, including porcini, morels and oyster mushrooms. They add a good flavour to a dish, but need to be reconstituted (soaked) before use.

Health and Nutrition

Vegetables contain many essential nutrients and are especially high in vitamins A, B and C. They contain important minerals, in particular iron and calcium, and are also low in fat, high in fibre and have low cholesterol value. Red and orange vegetables, such as peppers and carrots, and dark green vegetables, such as broccoli, contain excellent anti-cancer properties as well as helping to prevent heart disease. Current healthy eating guidelines suggest that at least five portions of fruit and vegetables should be eaten per day, with vegetables being the more essential.

Availability

There is a huge range of fresh vegetables on sale today in supermarkets, greengrocers and local markets. Also available is an ever-growing selection of fresh organic produce, plus a wide variety of seasonal pick-your-own vegetables from specialist farms. For enthusiastic gardeners, a vast range of vegetable seeds are available. In addition, the increase of ethnic markets has introduced an extensive choice of exotic vegetables, such as chayote and breadfruit.

With improved refrigeration and transport networks, vegetables are now flown around the world, resulting in year-round availability. Of course, you may want to do your best to stick to locally grown and seasonal food to avoid the higher environmental impact of imported and out-of-season vegetables.

Buying

When buying fresh vegetables, always look for ones that are bright and feel firm to the touch, and avoid any that are damaged or bruised. Choose onions and garlic that are hard and not sprouting; avoid ones that are soft, as they may be damaged. Salad leaves and other leaf vegetables should be fresh, bright and crisp – do not buy any that are wilted, look limp or have yellow leaves.

Storing

Many vegetables can be kept in a cool, dry, dark place, but some should be refrigerated.

∾ **Root vegetables, tubers and winter squashes** – These should be kept in a cool, dry, dark place that is free of frost, such as a larder or garage. Winter squashes can be kept for several months if stored correctly.

- **Green vegetables, fruit vegetables and salad leaves** – These should be kept in the salad drawer of the refrigerator.

- **Vegetables such as peas and beans** – These do not keep for very long, so try to eat them as soon as possible after buying or picking.

Preparing

Always clean vegetables thoroughly before using. Brush or scrape off any dirt and wash well in cold water. Prepare the vegetables just before cooking, as once peeled, they lose nutrients. Do not leave them in water, as valuable water-soluble vitamins will be lost.

- **Lettuce and other salad** – Wash leaves gently under cold running water and pull off and discard any tough stalks or outer leaves. Tear rather than cut the leaves. Dry thoroughly in a salad spinner or on paper towels before use, otherwise the leaves tend to wilt.

- **Spinach** – This should be washed thoroughly to remove all traces of dirt. Cut off and discard any tough stalks and damaged leaves.

- **Leeks** – These need to be thoroughly cleaned before use to remove any grit and dirt. After trimming the root and tough ends, make one cut lengthways (but not all the way along if you are intending to cook whole), and rinse under running water, getting right between the leaves.

- **Mushrooms** – Since mushrooms have a high water content, it is generally advised not to wash them, in order to avoid them absorbing even more water. Therefore, most mushrooms can just be wiped with paper towels or a damp cloth.

Cooking Techniques

Vegetables can be cooked in a variety of different ways, such as baking, barbecuing, blanching, boiling, braising, deep-frying, grilling, roasting, sautéing, steaming and stir-frying.

∾ Boiling – Always cook vegetables in a minimum amount of water and do not overcook, or valuable nutrients will be lost. It is best to cut vegetables into even-sized pieces and cook them briefly.

∾ Blanching and Parboiling – These mean lightly cooking raw vegetables for a brief period of time, whether parboiling potatoes before roasting, cooking cabbage before braising or cooking leaf vegetables such as spinach. Spinach should be cooked in only the water clinging to its leaves for 2–3 minutes until wilted.

Blanching is also used to remove skins easily from tomatoes. Cut a small cross in the top of the tomato and place in a heatproof bowl. Cover with boiling water and leave for a few seconds, then drain and peel off the skin.

∾ Braising – This method is a slow way of cooking certain vegetables, notably red or white cabbage. The vegetable is simmered for a long period of time in a small amount of stock or water.

∾ Steaming – This is a great way to cook vegetables such as broccoli, cauliflower, beans, carrots, parsnips and peas.

1. Cut the vegetables into even-sized pieces. Fill a large saucepan with about 5 cm/2 inches water, bring to the boil, then reduce to a simmer.

Vegetables & Salads

2. Place the vegetables in a metal steamer basket or colander and lower into the saucepan, then cover and steam until tender. Alternatively, use a plate standing on a trivet in the pan. Asparagus is traditionally cooked in an asparagus steamer. Do not let the water boil – it should just simmer.

3. Once tender, serve – there is no need to drain!

✍ Microwaving – Vegetables can be cooked very successfully in the microwave and retain all their flavour and nutrients as well as their colour.

1. Prepare the vegetables, cutting into even-sized pieces. Place in a microwaveable bowl or arrange in a shallow dish.

2. For firm vegetables such as root vegetables, add 1–3 tablespoons water and cover with microwaveable wrap. Pierce in a couple of places. Cook on high for 2–4 minutes, depending on how many vegetables and which variety is being cooked. The more delicate vegetables will require less cooking time and less water. Refer to the manufacturer's guidelines to be sure of times.

3. Remove from the oven and leave to stand for 1–2 minutes before serving. Do not season until after cooking, especially with salt, as this will toughen the vegetables.

✍ Grilling and Griddling – To grill peppers, cut in half or quarters and discard the seeds. Place, skin side uppermost on a foil-lined rack. Brush lightly with a little oil, then cook under the preheated grill for 5 minutes. Turn over, brush again and continue to grill for a further 3 minutes or until tender. Serve.

To grill aubergines, trim and wash, then either cut into slices or lengths. Brush lightly with a little oil and place on a foil-lined grill rack or in a hot griddle pan. Cook under the preheated grill or in the griddle pan for 3–5 minutes or until the aubergine has softened. Turn over, brush again and continue grilling for a further 3 minutes or until tender.

To grill tomatoes, rinse and cut in half. Place on a foil-lined grill rack and, if liked, season to taste. Cook under a preheated grill and cook for 3–5 minutes until cooked to personal preference.

❧ Grilling (to remove skins) – For peppers, aubergines and tomatoes, brush them with a little oil first, as they quickly dry out. To remove the skins from peppers:

1. Cut in half lengthways and deseed. Place skin-side up on the grill rack under a preheated hot grill and cook until the skins are blackened.

2. Remove with tongs and place in a polythene bag, which will retain moisture. Seal and leave for 8–10 minutes, until the peppers are cool enough to handle.

3. Once cool, remove from the bag and carefully peel away the blackened skin.

❧ Deep-frying – This method is suitable for most vegetables except leafy ones. The vegetables can be cut into small pieces, coated in batter, then deep-fried briefly in hot oil.

❧   Vegetables & Salads

~ Stir-frying – Stir-frying is an excellent way of serving all manner of vegetables. This way, all the nutrients are retained due to the short cooking time. Vegetables suitable for stir-frying include: peppers, courgettes, sugar snaps, beans, baby corn, carrots, pak choi, spinach, tiny broccoli florets, spring onions, and mushrooms, as well as sprouting seeds and shoots. To stir-fry:

1. Prepare all the vegetables before starting to cook. Peel, trim, then cut any large pieces of vegetables into thin strips.

2. Heat a wok for 1 minute, or until very hot, then add 1–2 tablespoons oil and carefully swirl the wok with the hot oil.

3. Add spices and flavours such as grated root ginger, chopped chilli and lemongrass and cook for 1 minute, then add the prepared vegetables, starting with the firmest, such as carrots.

4. Using a large spatula or spoon, stir-fry over a high heat, adding soy or other sauce as required. Cook for about 3–4 minutes, ensuring that the vegetables are still crisp.

~ Sweating – This method cooks vegetables such as onions in their own juices with or without a little oil. The vegetables should not be browned by this method and will retain masses of flavour and nutrients.

1. Prepare cleaned vegetables, cutting into small or medium-sized pieces.

2. Place in a frying pan or large saucepan and place over a low heat, with a little oil, if liked.

3. Cover with a lid and cook very gently in the steam that is generated. Stir occasionally. Use either in a casserole or as the basis for a soup or sauce.

∾ Caramelising Onions – This is very simple to do, but requires patience.

1. Peel the onions – and garlic, if using – and slice very thinly.

2. Melt a little unsalted butter in a heavy-based saucepan; you will need about 50 g/2 oz (4 tbsp) butter to 450 g/1 lb sliced onions.

3. Once the butter has melted, add the onions and garlic and cook very gently, stirring, until all the onions are coated in the butter. Continue to cook over a low heat, stirring occasionally with a wooden spoon.

4. If liked, 1 teaspoon sugar can be added, which will speed up the caramelising process. The onion will slowly soften and then begin to change colour and finally will caramelise. It will take anything from 15–30 minutes.

Some cooks advocate cooking for up to 1 hour. This gives an intense flavour, but great care must be taken that the onions do not disintegrate or burn. Use as the basis of a brown sauce or casserole.

∾ Roasting – Suitable for vegetables such as fennel, courgettes, pumpkin, squash, peppers, garlic, aubergines and tomatoes. Cut the vegetables into even-sized chunks. Heat some oil in a roasting tin in a preheated oven at 200°C/400°F/Gas Mark 6. Put the vegetables in the hot oil, baste and roast in the oven for 30 minutes. Garlic can be split into different cloves or whole heads can be roasted. It is best not to peel them until cooked.

Salads

Forget about thinking of salads as boring and unfilling – the salads in this section are unique, delicious and satisfying. They are perfect to use as sides or as a main dish that Goldilocks would love: not too heavy and not too light. Try the Bulgur Wheat Salad with Minty Lemon Dressing or the Spiced Couscous & Vegetables; they will wake up your taste buds in no time!

Winter Coleslaw

Serves 6

175 g/6 oz white cabbage
1 medium red onion, peeled
175 g/6 oz carrot, peeled
175 g/6 oz celeriac, peeled
2 celery stalks, trimmed
75 g/3 oz golden sultanas

For the yogurt and herb dressing:

150 ml/¼ pint low-fat natural yogurt
1 garlic clove, peeled and crushed
1 tbsp lemon juice
1 tsp clear honey
1 tbsp freshly snipped chives

Remove the hard core from the cabbage with a small knife and shred finely.

Slice the onion finely and coarsely grate the carrot.

Place the raw vegetables in a large bowl and mix together.

Cut the celeriac into thin strips and simmer in boiling water for about 2 minutes.

Drain the celeriac and rinse thoroughly with cold water.

Chop the celery and add to the bowl with the celeriac and sultanas and mix well.

Make the yogurt and herb dressing by briskly whisking the yogurt, garlic, lemon juice, honey and chives together.

Pour the dressing over the top of the salad. Stir the vegetables thoroughly to coat evenly and serve.

Spiced Couscous & Vegetables

Serves 4

1 tbsp olive oil
1 large shallot, peeled and
finely chopped
1 garlic clove, peeled and
finely chopped
1 small red pepper, deseeded and
cut into strips
1 small yellow pepper, deseeded
and cut into strips
1 small aubergine, diced
1 tsp each turmeric, ground cumin,
ground cinnamon and paprika
2 tsp ground coriander
large pinch saffron strands
2 tomatoes, peeled, deseeded
and diced
2 tbsp lemon juice
225 g/8 oz couscous
225 ml/8 fl oz vegetable stock
2 tbsp raisins
2 tbsp whole almonds
2 tbsp freshly chopped parsley
2 tbsp freshly chopped coriander
salt and freshly ground black pepper

Heat the oil in a large frying pan and add the shallot and garlic and cook for 2–3 minutes until softened. Add the peppers and aubergine and reduce the heat. Cook for 8–10 minutes until the vegetables are tender, adding a little water, if necessary.

Test a piece of aubergine to ensure it is cooked through. Add all the spices and cook for a further minute, stirring. Increase the heat and add the tomatoes and lemon juice. Cook for 2–3 minutes until the tomatoes have started to break down. Remove from the heat and leave to cool slightly.

Meanwhile, put the couscous into a large bowl. Bring the stock to the boil in a saucepan, then pour over the couscous. Stir well and cover with a clean tea towel.

Leave to stand for 7–8 minutes until all the stock is absorbed and the couscous is tender.

Uncover the couscous and fluff with a fork. Stir in the vegetable and spice mixture along with the raisins, almonds, parsley and coriander. Season to taste with salt and pepper and serve.

Bulgur Wheat Salad with Minty Lemon Dressing

Serves 4

125 g/4 oz bulghur wheat
10 cm /4 inch piece cucumber
2 shallots, peeled
125 g/4 oz baby sweetcorn
3 ripe but firm tomatoes

For the dressing:

grated zest of 1 lemon
3 tbsp lemon juice
3 tbsp freshly chopped mint
2 tbsp freshly
chopped parsley
1–2 tsp clear honey
2 tbsp sunflower oil
salt and freshly ground
black pepper

Place the bulgur wheat in a saucepan and cover with boiling water.

Simmer for about 10 minutes, then drain thoroughly and turn into a serving bowl.

Cut the cucumber into small dice, chop the shallots finely and reserve. Steam the sweetcorn over a pan of boiling water for 10 minutes, or until tender. Drain and slice into thick chunks.

Cut a cross in the top of each tomato and place in boiling water until their skins start to peel away.

Remove the skins and the seeds and cut the tomatoes into small dice.

Make the dressing by briskly whisking all the ingredients in a small bowl until mixed well.

When the bulgur wheat has cooled a little, add all the prepared vegetables and stir in the dressing. Season to taste with salt and pepper and serve.

Mediterranean Potato Salad

Serves 4

700 g/1¹/₂ lb small waxy potatoes
2 red onions, peeled and
roughly chopped
1 yellow pepper, deseeded and
roughly chopped
1 green pepper, deseeded and
roughly chopped
6 tbsp extra virgin olive oil
125 g/4 oz ripe tomatoes, chopped
50 g/2 oz pitted black olives, sliced
125 g/4 oz vegetarian feta cheese
3 tbsp freshly chopped parsley
2 tbsp white wine vinegar
1 tsp Dijon mustard
1 tsp clear honey
salt and freshly ground black pepper
fresh parsley sprigs, to garnish

Preheat the oven to 200°C/400°F/Gas Mark 6. Place the potatoes in a large saucepan of salted water, bring to the boil and simmer until just tender. Do not overcook. Drain and plunge into cold water to stop them from cooking further.

Place the onions in a bowl with the yellow and green peppers, then pour over 2 tablespoons of the olive oil. Stir and spoon onto a large baking tray. Cook in the preheated oven for 25–30 minutes until the vegetables are tender and lightly charred in places, stirring occasionally. Remove from the oven and transfer to a large bowl.

Cut the potatoes into bite-size pieces and mix with the roasted onions and peppers. Add the tomatoes and olives to the potatoes. Crumble over the feta cheese and sprinkle with the chopped parsley.

Whisk together the remaining olive oil, vinegar, mustard and honey, then season to taste with salt and pepper. Pour the dressing over the potatoes and toss gently together. Garnish with parsley sprigs and serve immediately.

Mediterranean Rice Salad

Serves 4

250 g/9 oz Camargue red rice
2 sun-dried tomatoes,
finely chopped
2 garlic cloves, peeled and
finely chopped
4 tbsp oil from a jar of sun-dried
tomatoes
2 tsp balsamic vinegar
2 tsp red wine vinegar
salt and freshly ground
black pepper
1 red onion, peeled and thinly sliced
1 yellow pepper, quartered
and deseeded
1 red pepper, quartered
and deseeded

$^{1}/_{2}$ cucumber, peeled and diced
6 ripe plum tomatoes, cut
into wedges
1 fennel bulb, halved and
thinly sliced
fresh basil leaves, to garnish

Cook the rice in a saucepan of lightly salted boiling water for 35–40 minutes until tender. Drain well and reserve.

Whisk the sun-dried tomatoes, garlic, oil and vinegars together in a small bowl or jug. Season to taste with salt and pepper. Put the red onion in a large bowl, pour over the dressing and leave to allow the flavours to develop.

Put the peppers skin-side up on a grill rack and cook under a preheated hot grill for 5–6 minutes until blackened and charred. Remove and place in a plastic bag. When cool enough to handle, peel off the skins and slice the peppers.

Add the peppers, cucumber, tomatoes, fennel and rice to the onions. Mix gently together to coat in the dressing. Cover and chill in the refrigerator for 30 minutes to allow the flavours to mingle.

Remove the salad from the refrigerator and leave to stand at room temperature for 20 minutes. Garnish with fresh basil leaves and serve.

Tortellini & Summer Vegetable Salad

Serves 6

350 g/12 oz mixed green and plain cheese-filled fresh tortellini
150 ml/¹/₄ pint extra virgin olive oil
225 g/8 oz fine green beans, trimmed
175 g/6 oz broccoli florets
1 yellow or red pepper, deseeded and thinly sliced
1 red onion, peeled and sliced
175 g jar marinated artichoke hearts, drained and halved
2 tbsp capers
75 g/3 oz dry-cured, pitted black olives
3 tbsp raspberry or balsamic vinegar
1 tbsp Dijon mustard
1 tsp soft brown sugar
salt and freshly ground black pepper
2 tbsp freshly chopped basil or flat-leaf parsley
2 quartered hard-boiled eggs, to garnish

Bring a large pan of lightly salted water to a rolling boil. Add the tortellini and cook according to the packet instructions, or until *al dente*. Using a large slotted spoon, transfer the tortellini to a colander to drain. Rinse under cold running water and drain again. Transfer to a large bowl and toss with 2 tablespoons of the olive oil.

Return the pasta water to the boil and drop in the green beans and broccoli florets; blanch them for 2 minutes, or until just beginning to soften. Drain, rinse under cold running water and drain again thoroughly. Add the vegetables to the reserved tortellini.

Add the pepper, onion, artichoke hearts, capers and olives to the bowl. Stir lightly.

Whisk together the vinegar, mustard and brown sugar in a bowl and season to taste with salt and pepper. Slowly whisk in the remaining olive oil to form a thick, creamy dressing. Pour over the tortellini and vegetables, add the chopped basil or parsley and stir until lightly coated. Transfer to a shallow serving dish or salad bowl. Garnish with the hard-boiled egg quarters and serve.

Baby Roast Potato Salad

Serves 4

350 g/12 oz small shallots
900 g/2 lb small even-sized
new potatoes
2 tbsp olive oil
sea salt and freshly ground
black pepper
2 medium courgettes
175 g/6 oz cherry tomatoes
2 fresh rosemary sprigs
150 ml/¼ pint soured cream
2 tbsp freshly snipped chives

Preheat the oven to 200°C/400°F/Gas Mark 6. Trim the shallots, but leave the skins on. Put in a saucepan of lightly salted boiling water with the potatoes and cook for 5 minutes, then drain. Separate the shallots and plunge them into cold water for 1 minute.

Put the oil on a baking sheet lined with kitchen foil or a roasting tin and heat for a few minutes. Peel the skins off the shallots – they should now come away easily. Add to the baking sheet or roasting tin with the potatoes and toss in the oil to coat. Sprinkle with a little sea salt. Roast the potatoes and shallots in the preheated oven for 10 minutes.

Meanwhile, trim the courgettes, halve lengthways and cut into 5 cm/ 2 inch chunks. Add to the baking sheet or roasting tin, toss to mix and cook for 5 minutes.

Pierce the tomato skins with a sharp knife. Add to the sheet or tin with the rosemary and cook for a further 5 minutes, or until all the vegetables are tender. Remove the rosemary and discard. Grind a little black pepper over the vegetables.

Spoon into a wide serving bowl. Mix together the sour cream and chives and drizzle over the vegetables just before serving.

Oriental Noodle & Peanut Salad with Coriander

Serves 4

350 g/12 oz rice vermicelli
1 litre/1³/₄ pints
vegetable stock
2 tsp sesame oil
2 tbsp light soy sauce
8 spring onions
3 tbsp groundnut oil
2 hot green chillis, deseeded and
thinly sliced
25 g/1 oz roughly chopped coriander
2 tbsp freshly chopped mint
125 g/4 oz cucumber,
finely chopped
40 g/1¹/₂ oz beansprouts
40 g/1¹/₂ oz roasted peanuts,
roughly chopped

Put the noodles into a large bowl. Bring the stock to the boil and immediately pour over the noodles. Leave to soak for 4 minutes, or according to the packet instructions. Drain well, discarding the stock or saving it for another use. Mix together the sesame oil and soy sauce and pour over the hot noodles. Toss well to coat and leave until cold.

Trim and thinly slice 4 of the spring onions. Heat the groundnut oil in a wok over a low heat. Add the spring onions and, as soon as they sizzle, remove from the heat and leave to cool. When cold, toss with the noodles.

On a chopping board, cut the remaining spring onions lengthways four to six times, leave in a bowl of cold water until tassels form. Serve the noodles in individual bowls, each dressed with a little chilli, coriander, mint, cucumber, beansprouts and peanuts. Garnish with the spring onion tassels and serve.

Warm Noodle Salad with Sesame & Peanut Dressing

Serves 4–6

125 g/4 oz smooth peanut butter
6 tbsp sesame oil
3 tbsp light soy sauce
2 tbsp red wine vinegar
1 tbsp freshly grated root ginger
2 tbsp double cream
250 g pack Chinese fine egg noodles
125 g/4 oz beansprouts
225 g/8 oz baby sweetcorn
125 g/4 oz carrots, peeled and cut into matchsticks
125 g/4 oz mangetout
125 g/4 oz cucumber, cut into thin strips
3 spring onions, trimmed and finely shredded

Place the peanut butter, 4 tablespoons of the sesame oil, the soy sauce, vinegar and ginger in a food processor. Blend until smooth, then stir in 85 ml/3 fl oz hot water and blend again. Pour in the cream, blend briefly until smooth. Pour the dressing into a jug and reserve.

Bring a saucepan of lightly salted water to the boil, add the noodles and beansprouts and cook for 4 minutes, or according to the packet instructions. Drain, rinse under cold running water and drain again. Stir in the remaining sesame oil and keep warm.

Bring a saucepan of lightly salted water to the boil and add the baby sweetcorn, carrots and mangetout and cook for 3–4 minutes until just tender but still crisp. Drain and cut the mangetout in half. Slice the baby sweetcorn (if very large) into 2–3 pieces and arrange on a warm serving dish with the noodles. Add the cucumber strips and spring onions. Spoon over a little of the dressing and serve immediately with the remaining dressing.

Cooked Vegetable Salad with Satay Sauce

Serves 4

125 ml/4 fl oz groundnut oil
225 g/8 oz unsalted peanuts
1 onion, peeled and finely chopped
1 garlic clove, peeled and crushed
1/2 tsp chilli powder
1 tsp ground coriander
1/2 tsp each ground cumin and sugar
1 tbsp dark soy sauce
2 tbsp fresh lemon juice
2 tbsp light olive oil
salt and freshly ground black pepper
125 g/4 oz French green beans, trimmed and halved
125 g/4 oz carrots
125 g/4 oz cauliflower florets
125 g/4 oz broccoli florets
125 g/4 oz Chinese leaves or pak choi, trimmed and shredded
125 g/4 oz beansprouts
1 tbsp sesame oil
fresh watercress sprigs and cucumber slivers, to garnish

Heat a wok, add the oil and, when hot, add the peanuts and stir-fry for 3–4 minutes. Drain on absorbent kitchen paper and leave to cool. Blend in a food processor to a fine powder.

Place the onion and garlic with the spices, sugar, soy sauce, lemon juice and olive oil in a food processor. Season to taste with salt and pepper, then process into a paste. Transfer to a wok and stir-fry for 3–4 minutes.

Stir 600 ml/1 pint hot water into the paste and bring to the boil. Add the ground peanuts and simmer gently for 5–6 minutes until the mixture thickens. Reserve the satay sauce.

Cook in batches, in lightly salted boiling water, the French beans, carrots, cauliflower and broccoli for 3–4 minutes, and the Chinese leaves or pak choi and beansprouts for 2 minutes. Drain each batch, drizzle over the sesame oil and arrange on a large, warm serving dish. Garnish with watercress sprigs and cucumber. Serve with the satay sauce.

Panzanella

Serves 4

250 g/9 oz day-old Italian-style bread
1 tbsp red wine vinegar
4 tbsp olive oil
1 tsp lemon juice
1 small garlic clove, peeled and
finely chopped
1 red onion, peeled and finely sliced
1 cucumber, peeled if preferred
225 g/8 oz ripe tomatoes, deseeded
150 g/5 oz pitted black olives
about 20 basil leaves, coarsely torn,
or left whole if small
sea salt and freshly ground
black pepper

Cut the bread into thick slices, leaving the crusts on. Add 1 teaspoon of the red wine vinegar to a jug of iced water, put the slices of bread in a bowl and pour over the water. Make sure the bread is covered completely. Leave to soak for 3–4 minutes until just soft.

Remove the soaked bread from the water and squeeze it gently, first with your hands and then in a clean tea towel to remove any excess water. Put the bread on a plate, cover with clingfilm and chill in the refrigerator for about 1 hour.

Meanwhile, whisk together the olive oil, the remaining red wine vinegar and lemon juice in a large serving bowl. Add the garlic and onion and stir to coat well.

Halve the cucumber and remove the seeds. Chop both the cucumber and tomatoes into 1 cm/$^{1}/_{2}$ inch dice. Add to the garlic and onion with the olives. Tear the bread into bite-size chunks and add to the bowl with the fresh basil leaves. Toss together to mix and serve immediately with a grinding of sea salt and black pepper.

Starters
& Sides

The recipes in this section are a great way to set the tone for a nice meal – they taste wonderful and will make you seem like a top chef! Of course, they're good enough to have for a light meal too... Whether starters or sides, they are perfect accompaniments to a main dish, but be careful: they're so good, you might forget that the rest of the meal is there!

Spanish Baked Tomatoes

Serves 4

175 g/6 oz wholegrain rice
600 ml/1 pint vegetable stock
2 tsp sunflower oil
2 shallots, peeled and
finely chopped
1 garlic clove, peeled
and crushed
1 green pepper, deseeded and
cut into small dice
1 red chilli, deseeded and
finely chopped
50 g/2 oz button mushrooms,
finely chopped
1 tbsp freshly
chopped oregano
salt and freshly ground
black pepper
4 large, ripe beef tomatoes
1 large egg, beaten
1 tsp caster sugar
basil leaves, to garnish
crusty bread, to serve

Preheat the oven to 180°C/350°F/Gas Mark 4. Place the rice in a saucepan, pour over the vegetable stock and bring to the boil. Simmer for 30 minutes, or until the rice is tender. Drain and turn into a mixing bowl.

Add 1 teaspoon of the sunflower oil to a small, nonstick pan and gently fry the shallots, garlic, pepper, chilli and mushrooms for 2 minutes. Add to the rice with the chopped oregano. Season with plenty of salt and pepper.

Slice the top off each tomato. Cut and scoop out the flesh, removing the hard core. Pass the tomato flesh through a sieve. Add 1 tablespoon of the juice to the rice mixture. Stir in the beaten egg and mix. Sprinkle a little sugar in the base of each tomato. Pile the rice mixture into the shells.

Place the tomatoes in a baking dish and pour a little cold water around them. Replace their lids and drizzle a few drops of the sunflower oil over the tops.

Bake in the preheated oven for about 25 minutes. Garnish with the basil leaves, season with black pepper and serve immediately with crusty bread.

Stuffed Onions with Pine Nuts

Serves 4

4 medium onions, peeled
2 garlic cloves, peeled
and crushed
2 tbsp fresh brown breadcrumbs
4 tbsp white breadcrumbs
25 g/1 oz sultanas
25 g/1 oz pine nuts
50 g/2 oz low-fat hard cheese such
as Edam, grated
2 tbsp freshly chopped parsley
salt and freshly ground
black pepper
1 medium egg, beaten
salad leaves, to serve

Preheat the oven to 200°C/400°F/Gas Mark 6. Bring a pan of water to the boil, add the onions and cook gently for about 15 minutes.

Drain the onions well. Allow them to cool, then slice each one in half horizontally.

Scoop out most of the onion flesh, but leave a reasonably firm shell.

Chop up 4 tablespoons of the onion flesh and place in a bowl with the crushed garlic, brown breadcrumbs, 2 tablespoons of the white breadcrumbs, sultanas, pine nuts, grated cheese and parsley.

Mix the breadcrumb mixture together thoroughly and season to taste with salt and pepper. Bind together with as much of the beaten egg as necessary to make a firm filling.

Pile the mixture back into the onion shells and top with the remaining breadcrumbs. Place on a oiled baking tray and cook in the preheated oven for 20–30 minutes until golden brown. Serve immediately with the salad leaves.

Savoury Wontons

Serves 15

125 g/4 oz filo pastry or wonton skins
15 whole chive leaves
25 g/1 oz butter
225 g/8 oz spinach
1/2 tsp salt
225 g/8 oz mushrooms, wiped and
roughly chopped
1 garlic clove, peeled and crushed
1–2 tbsp dark soy sauce
2.5 cm/1 inch piece fresh root
ginger, peeled and grated
salt and freshly ground
black pepper
1 small egg, beaten
300 ml/1/2 pint groundnut oil,
for deep-frying

To garnish:

spring onion curls
radish roses

Cut the filo pastry or wonton skins into 12.5 cm/5 inch squares, stack and cover with clingfilm. Chill in the refrigerator while preparing the filling. Blanch the chive leaves in boiling water for 1 minute, drain and reserve.

Melt the butter in a saucepan, add the spinach and salt and cook for 2–3 minutes until wilted. Add the mushrooms and garlic and cook for 2–3 minutes until tender.

Transfer the spinach and mushroom mixture to a bowl. Stir in the soy sauce and ginger. Season to taste with salt and pepper.

Place a small spoonful of the spinach and mushroom mixture onto a pastry or wonton square and brush the edges with beaten egg. Gather up the four corners to make a little bag and tie with a chive leaf. Make up the remainder of the wontons.

Heat a wok, add the oil and heat to 180°C/350°F. Deep-fry the wontons in batches for 2–3 minutes until golden and crisp. Drain on absorbent kitchen paper and serve immediately, garnished with spring onion curls and radish roses.

Sweetcorn Fritters

Serves 4

4 tbsp groundnut oil
1 small onion, peeled
and finely chopped
1 red chilli, deseeded
and finely chopped
1 garlic clove, peeled
and crushed
1 tsp ground coriander
325 g can sweetcorn
6 spring onions, trimmed and
finely sliced
1 medium egg, lightly beaten
salt and freshly ground
black pepper
3 tbsp plain flour
1 tsp baking powder
spring onion curls, to garnish
Thai-style chutney, to serve

Heat 1 tablespoon of the groundnut oil in a frying pan, add the onion and cook gently for 7–8 minutes until beginning to soften. Add the chilli, garlic and ground coriander and cook for 1 minute, stirring continuously. Remove from the heat.

Drain the sweetcorn and tip into a mixing bowl. Lightly mash with a potato masher to break down the corn a little. Add the cooked onion mixture to the bowl with the spring onions and beaten egg. Season to taste with salt and pepper, then stir to mix together. Sift the flour and baking powder over the mixture and stir in.

Heat 2 tablespoons of the groundnut oil in a large frying pan. Drop 4 or 5 heaped teaspoonfuls of the sweetcorn mixture into the pan and, using a fish slice or spatula, flatten each to make a 1 cm/½ inch thick fritter. Fry the fritters for 3 minutes, or until golden brown on the underside, turn over and fry for a further 3 minutes, or until cooked through and crisp.

Remove the fritters from the pan and drain on absorbent kitchen paper. Keep warm while cooking the remaining fritters, adding a little more oil if needed. Garnish with spring onion curls and serve immediately with a Thai-style chutney.

Roasted Aubergine Dip with Pitta Strips

Serves 4

4 pitta breads
2 large aubergines
1 garlic clove, peeled
¼ tsp sesame oil
1 tbsp lemon juice
½ tsp ground cumin
salt and freshly ground
black pepper
2 tbsp freshly chopped parsley
fresh salad leaves, to serve

Preheat the oven to 180°C/350°F/Gas Mark 4. On a chopping board, cut the pitta breads into strips. Spread the bread in a single layer onto a large baking tray. Cook in the preheated oven for 15 minutes until golden and crisp. Leave to cool on a wire cooling rack.

Trim the aubergines, rinse lightly and reserve. Heat a griddle pan until almost smoking. Cook the aubergines and garlic for about 15 minutes. Turn frequently until very tender with wrinkled and charred skins. Remove from the heat. Leave to cool.

When the aubergines are cool enough to handle, cut in half and scoop out the cooked flesh and place in a food processor.

Squeeze the softened garlic flesh from the papery skin and add to the aubergine.

Blend the aubergine and garlic until smooth, then add the sesame oil, lemon juice and cumin and blend again to mix. Season to taste with salt and pepper, stir in the parsley and serve with the pitta strips and mixed salad leaves.

Onion Bhajis

Serves 4–6

2 large onions, peeled
225 g/8 oz chickpea flour
small piece fresh root ginger,
peeled and grated
^{1}/$_2$–1 small chilli, deseeded and
finely chopped
^{1}/$_2$ tsp turmeric
½ tsp ground coriander
4 tbsp freshly chopped coriander
freshly milled salt, to taste
125–150 ml/4–5 fl oz water
vegetable oil, for deep-frying

Finely slice the onions and place in a mixing bowl with the flour, spices and coriander. Add salt to taste.

Slowly stir in the water and mix to form a thick consistency. Form into loose balls.

Heat the oil in a deep-fryer to a temperature of 180°C/350°F. Drop the bhajis, about two or three at a time, into the hot oil and deep-fry for 2–3 minutes until golden brown and crisp. Remove with a slotted spoon and drain on absorbent kitchen paper. Serve.

Mozzarella Parcels with Cranberry Relish

Serves 6

125 g/4 oz vegetarian
mozzarella cheese
8 slices thin white bread
2 medium eggs, beaten
salt and freshly ground
black pepper
300 ml/½ pint olive oil

For the relish:

125 g/4 oz cranberries
2 tbsp fresh orange juice
grated zest of 1 small orange
50 g/2 oz soft light brown sugar
1 tbsp port

Slice the mozzarella thinly, remove the crusts from the bread and make sandwiches with the bread and cheese. Cut into 5 cm/2 inch squares and squash them quite flat. Season the eggs with salt and pepper, then soak the bread in the seasoned egg for 1 minute on each side until well coated.

Heat the oil to 190˚C/375˚F and deep-fry the bread squares for 1–2 minutes until they are crisp and golden brown. Drain on absorbent kitchen paper and keep warm while the cranberry relish is prepared.

Place the cranberries, orange juice, zest, sugar and port into a small saucepan and add 5 tablespoons water. Bring to the boil, then simmer for 10 minutes, or until the cranberries have 'popped'. Sweeten with a little more sugar if necessary.

Arrange the mozzarella parcels on individual serving plates. Serve with a little of the cranberry relish.

Sweet Potato Cakes with Mango & Tomato Salsa

Serves 4

700 g/1¹/₂ lb sweet potatoes, peeled
and cut into large chunks
25 g/1 oz butter
1 onion, peeled and chopped
1 garlic clove, peeled and crushed
pinch freshly grated nutmeg
salt and freshly ground
black pepper
1 medium egg, beaten
50 g/2 oz quick-cook polenta
2 tbsp sunflower oil

For the salsa:

1 ripe mango, peeled, stoned
and diced
6 cherry tomatoes, cut into wedges
4 spring onions, trimmed and
thinly sliced
1 red chilli, deseeded
and finely chopped
finely grated zest and juice of ¹/₂ lime
2 tbsp freshly chopped mint
1 tsp clear honey
salad leaves, to serve

Steam or cook the sweet potatoes in lightly salted boiling water for 15–20 minutes until tender. Drain well, then mash until smooth.

Melt the butter in a saucepan. Add the onion and garlic and cook gently for 10 minutes until soft. Add to the mashed sweet potato and season with the nutmeg, salt and pepper. Stir together until mixed thoroughly. Leave to cool.

Shape the mixture into four oval potato cakes, about 2.5 cm/1 inch thick. Dip first in the beaten egg, allowing the excess to fall back into the bowl, then coat in the polenta. Refrigerate for at least 30 minutes.

Meanwhile, mix together all the ingredients for the salsa. Spoon into a serving bowl, cover with clingfilm and leave at room temperature to allow the flavours to develop.

Heat the oil in a frying pan and cook the potato cakes for 4–5 minutes on each side. Serve with the salsa and salad leaves..

Hot Herby Mushrooms

Serves 4

4 thin slices white bread,
crusts removed
125 g/4 oz chestnut mushrooms,
wiped and sliced
125 g/4 oz oyster
mushrooms, wiped
1 garlic clove, peeled and crushed
1 tsp Dijon mustard
300 ml/½ pint vegetable stock
salt and freshly ground
black pepper
1 tbsp freshly chopped parsley
1 tbsp freshly snipped chives, plus
extra to garnish
mixed salad leaves,
to serve

Preheat the oven to 180˚C/350˚F/Gas Mark 4. With a rolling pin, roll each piece of bread out as thinly as possible. Press each piece of bread into a 10 cm/4 inch tartlet tin. Push each piece firmly down, then bake in the preheated oven for 20 minutes.

Place the mushrooms in a frying pan with the garlic, mustard and stock and stir-fry over a moderate heat until the mushrooms are tender and the liquid is reduced by half. Carefully remove the mushrooms from the frying pan with a slotted spoon and transfer to a heat-resistant dish. Cover with kitchen foil and place in the bottom of the oven to keep the mushrooms warm.

Boil the remaining pan juices until reduced to a thick sauce. Season with salt and pepper.

Stir the parsley and the chives into the mushroom mixture.

Place one bread tartlet case on each plate and divide the mushroom mixture between them.

Spoon over the pan juices, garnish with the chives and serve immediately with mixed salad leaves.

Crispy Pancake Rolls

Serves 8

250 g/9 oz plain flour
pinch salt
1 medium egg
4 tsp sunflower oil
2 tbsp light olive oil
2 cm/³/₄ inch piece fresh root
ginger, peeled and grated
1 garlic clove, peeled and crushed
225 g/8 oz tofu, drained and cut
into small dice
2 tbsp soy sauce
1 tbsp dry sherry
175 g/6 oz button mushrooms,
wiped and chopped
1 celery stalk, trimmed and
finely chopped
2 spring onions, trimmed and
finely chopped
2 tbsp groundnut oil
fresh coriander sprig and chopped
spring onion, to garnish

Sift 225 g/8 oz of the flour with the salt into a large bowl, make a well in the centre and drop in the egg. Beat to form a smooth, thin batter, gradually adding 300 ml/½ pint water and drawing in the flour from the sides of the bowl. Mix the remaining flour with 1–2 tablespoons water to make a thick paste. Reserve.

Heat a little sunflower oil in a 20.5 cm/8 inch omelette or frying pan and pour in 2 tablespoons of the batter. Cook for 1–2 minutes, flip over and cook for a further 1–2 minutes until firm. Slide from the pan and keep warm. Make more pancakes with the remaining batter.

Heat a wok or large frying pan, add the olive oil and, when hot, add the ginger, garlic and tofu, stir-fry for 30 seconds, then pour in the soy sauce and sherry. Add the mushrooms, celery and spring onions. Stir-fry for 1–2 minutes, then remove from the wok and leave to cool.

Place a little filling in the centre of each pancake. Brush the edges with the flour paste, fold in the edges, then roll up into parcels. Heat the groundnut oil to 180°C/350°F in the wok. Fry the pancake rolls for 2–3 minutes until golden. Serve immediately, garnished with chopped spring onions and a sprig of coriander.

Thai Stuffed Eggs with Spinach & Sesame Seeds

Serves 8

4 large eggs
salt and freshly ground
black pepper
225 g/8 oz baby spinach
2 garlic cloves, peeled and crushed
1 tbsp spring onions, trimmed and
finely chopped
1 tbsp sesame seeds
75 g/3 oz plain flour
1 tbsp light olive oil
300 ml/¹/₂ pint vegetable oil,
for frying

To garnish:

sliced red chilli
snipped fresh chives

Bring a small saucepan of water to the boil, add the eggs, bring back to the boil and cook for 6–7 minutes. Plunge into cold water, then shell and cut in half lengthways. Using a teaspoon, remove the yolks and place in a bowl. Reserve the whites.

Place 1 teaspoon water and ¹/₂ teaspoon salt in a saucepan, add the spinach and cook until tender and wilted. Drain, squeeze out the excess moisture and chop. Mix with the egg yolk, then stir in the garlic, spring onions and sesame seeds. Season to taste with salt and pepper. Fill the egg shells with the mixture, smoothing into a mound.

Place the flour in a bowl with the olive oil, a large pinch salt and 125 ml/4 fl oz warm water. Beat together to make a completely smooth batter.

Heat a wok, add the vegetable oil and heat to 180°C/350°F. Dip the stuffed eggs in the batter, allowing any excess batter to drip back into the bowl, and deep-fry in batches for 3–4 minutes until golden brown. Place the eggs in the wok filled-side down first, then turn over to finish cooking. Remove from the wok with a slotted spoon and drain on absorbent kitchen paper. Serve hot or cold, garnished with snipped chives and chilli rings.

Ginger & Garlic Potatoes

Serves 4

700 g/1¹/2 lb potatoes
2.5 cm/1 inch piece root ginger,
peeled and roughly chopped
3 garlic cloves, peeled and chopped
¹/2 tsp turmeric
1 tsp salt
¹/2 tsp cayenne pepper
5 tbsp vegetable oil
1 tsp whole fennel seeds
1 large eating apple, cored
and diced
6 spring onions, trimmed and
diagonally sliced
1 tbsp freshly chopped coriander

To serve:

assorted bitter salad leaves
curry-flavoured mayonnaise

Scrub the potatoes, then place, unpeeled, in a large saucepan and cover with boiling salted water. Bring to the boil and cook for 15 minutes, then drain and leave the potatoes to cool completely. Peel and cut into 2.5 cm/1 inch cubes.

Place the root ginger, garlic, turmeric, salt and cayenne pepper in a food processor and blend for 1 minute. With the motor still running, slowly add 3 tablespoons water and blend into a paste. Alternatively, pound the ingredients to a paste with a pestle and mortar.

Heat the oil in a large, heavy-based frying pan and, when hot but not smoking, add the fennel seeds and fry for a few minutes. Stir in the ginger paste and cook for 2 minutes, stirring frequently. Take care not to burn the mixture.

Reduce the heat, then add the potatoes and cook for 5–7 minutes, stirring frequently, until the potatoes have a golden-brown crust. Add the diced apple and spring onions, then sprinkle with the freshly chopped coriander. Heat through for 2 minutes, then serve on assorted salad leaves with curry-flavoured mayonnaise.

Roasted Mixed Vegetables with Garlic & Herb Sauce

Serves 4

1 large garlic bulb
1 large onion, peeled and cut into wedges
4 small carrots, peeled and quartered
4 small parsnips, peeled
6 small potatoes, scrubbed and halved
1 fennel bulb, thickly sliced
4 fresh rosemary sprigs
4 fresh thyme sprigs
2 tbsp olive oil
salt and freshly ground black pepper
200 g/7 oz low-fat soft cheese with herbs and garlic
4 tbsp milk
zest of 1/2 lemon
thyme sprigs, to garnish

Preheat the oven to 220°C/425°F/Gas Mark 7. Cut the garlic in half horizontally. Put into a large roasting tin with all the vegetables and herbs.

Add the oil, season well with salt and pepper and toss together to coat lightly in the oil.

Cover with kitchen foil and roast in the preheated oven for 50 minutes. Remove the foil and cook for a further 30 minutes until all the vegetables are tender and slightly charred.

Remove the tin from the oven and allow to cool.

In a small saucepan, melt the low-fat soft cheese together with the milk and lemon zest.

Remove the garlic from the roasting tin and squeeze the flesh into a bowl. Mash thoroughly, then add to the sauce. Heat through gently. Season the vegetables to taste. Pour some sauce into small ramekins and garnish with thyme sprigs. Serve immediately with the roasted vegetables and the sauce to dip.

Roasted Butternut Squash

Serves 4

2 small butternut squash
4 garlic cloves, peeled and crushed
1 tbsp olive oil
salt and freshly ground
black pepper
1 tbsp walnut oil
4 medium leeks, trimmed, cleaned
and thinly sliced
1 tbsp black mustard seeds
300 g can cannellini beans, drained
and rinsed
125 g/4 oz fine French beans, halved
150 ml/¹/₄ pint vegetable stock
50 g/2 oz rocket
2 tbsp freshly snipped chives
fresh chives, to garnish

To serve:

4 tbsp fromage frais
mixed salad

Preheat the oven to 200°C/400°F/Gas Mark 6. Cut the butternut squash in half lengthways and scoop out all of the seeds.

Score the squash in a diamond pattern with a sharp knife. Mix the garlic with the olive oil and brush over the cut surfaces of the squash. Season well with salt and pepper. Put on a baking sheet and roast for 40 minutes until tender.

Heat the walnut oil in a saucepan and fry the leeks and mustard seeds for 5 minutes.

Add the drained cannellini beans, French beans and vegetable stock. Bring to the boil and simmer gently for 5 minutes until the French beans are tender.

Remove from the heat and stir in the rocket and chives. Season well. Remove the squash from the oven and allow to cool for 5 minutes. Spoon in the bean mixture. Garnish with a few snipped chives and serve immediately with the fromage frais and a mixed salad.

Layered Cheese & Herb Potato Cake

Serves 4

900 g/2 lb waxy potatoes
3 tbsp freshly snipped chives
2 tbsp freshly chopped parsley
225 g/8 oz mature vegetarian
cheddar cheese
2 large egg yolks
1 tsp paprika
125 g/4 oz fresh white breadcrumbs
50 g/2 oz almonds, toasted and
roughly chopped
salt and freshly ground
black pepper
50 g/2 oz butter, melted
mixed salad or steamed vegetables,
to serve

Preheat the oven to 180°C/350°F/Gas Mark 4. Lightly oil and line the base of a 20.5 cm/ 8 inch round cake tin with lightly oiled greaseproof paper or baking parchment. Peel and thinly slice the potatoes and reserve. Stir the chives, parsley, cheese and egg yolks together in a small bowl and reserve. Mix the paprika into the breadcrumbs.

Sprinkle the almonds over the base of the lined tin. Cover with half the potatoes, arranging them in layers, then sprinkle with the paprika breadcrumb mixture and season to taste with salt and pepper.

Spoon the cheese and herb mixture over the breadcrumbs with a little more seasoning, then arrange the remaining potatoes on top. Drizzle over the melted butter and press the surface down firmly.

Bake in the preheated oven for 1¼ hours, or until golden and cooked through. Let the tin stand for 10 minutes before carefully turning out and serving in thick wedges. Serve immediately with salad or freshly cooked vegetables.

Vegetables Braised in Olive Oil & Lemon

Serves 4

small strip pared zest and juice
of 1/2 lemon
4 tbsp olive oil
1 bay leaf
large thyme sprig
150 ml/1/4 pint water
4 spring onions, trimmed and
finely chopped
175 g/6 oz baby button mushrooms
175 g/6 oz broccoli,
cut into small florets
175 g/6 oz cauliflower, cut into
small florets
1 medium courgette,
sliced on the diagonal
2 tbsp freshly snipped chives
salt and freshly ground
black pepper
lemon zest, to garnish

Put the pared lemon zest and juice into a large saucepan. Add the olive oil, bay leaf, thyme and the water. Bring to the boil. Add the spring onions and mushrooms. Top with the broccoli and cauliflower, trying to add them so that the stalks are submerged in the water and the tops are just above it. Cover and simmer for 3 minutes.

Scatter the courgette on top, so that the slices are steamed rather than boiled. Cook, covered, for a further 3–4 minutes until all the vegetables are tender. Using a slotted spoon, transfer the vegetables from the liquid into a warm serving dish. Increase the heat and boil rapidly for 3–4 minutes until the liquid is reduced to about 8 tablespoons. Remove the lemon rind, bay leaf and thyme sprig and discard.

Stir the chives into the reduced liquid, season to taste with salt and pepper and pour over the vegetables. Sprinkle with lemon zest and serve immediately.

Coconut-baked Courgettes

Serves 4

3 tbsp groundnut oil
1 onion, peeled and finely sliced
4 garlic cloves, peeled and crushed
$^1/_2$ tsp chilli powder
1 tsp ground coriander
6–8 tbsp desiccated coconut
1 tbsp tomato purée
700 g/1$^1/_2$ lb courgettes, thinly sliced
freshly chopped parsley, to garnish

Preheat the oven to 180°C/350°F/Gas Mark 4, 10 minutes before cooking. Lightly oil a 1.5 litre/2$^1/_2$ pint ovenproof gratin dish. Heat a wok, add the oil and, when hot, add the onion and stir-fry for 2–3 minutes until softened. Add the garlic, chilli powder and coriander and stir-fry for 1–2 minutes.

Pour 300 ml/½ pint cold water into the wok and bring to the boil. Add the coconut and tomato purée and simmer for 3–4 minutes; most of the water will evaporate at this stage. Spoon 4 tablespoons of the spice and coconut mixture into a small bowl and reserve.

Stir the courgettes into the remaining spice and coconut mixture, coating well. Spoon the courgettes into the oiled gratin dish and sprinkle the reserved spice and coconut mixture evenly over the top. Bake, uncovered, in the preheated oven for 15–20 minutes until golden. Garnish with chopped parsley and serve immediately.

Soups & Stews

Most people don't think of soups as versatile, but in this section, you'll find perfect recipes for every occasion. The Tomato & Basil soup makes a great light first course, but the Italian Bean Soup and the Mushroom Stew are hearty enough to be a delightful meal on their own.

Swede, Turnip, Parsnip & Potato Soup

Serves 4

2 large onions, peeled
25 g/1 oz butter
2 medium carrots, peeled and roughly chopped
175 g/6 oz swede, peeled and roughly chopped
125 g/4 oz turnip, peeled and roughly chopped
125 g/4 oz parsnips, peeled and roughly chopped
175 g/6 oz potatoes, peeled
1 litre/1³/₄ pints vegetable stock
¹/₂ tsp freshly grated nutmeg
salt and freshly ground black pepper
4 tbsp vegetable oil, for frying
125 ml/4 fl oz double cream
warm crusty bread, to serve

Finely chop 1 onion. Melt the butter in a large saucepan and add the onion, carrots, swede, turnip, parsnip and potatoes. Cover and cook gently for about 10 minutes, without colouring. Stir occasionally during this time.

Add the stock and season to taste with the nutmeg, salt and pepper. Cover and bring to the boil, then reduce the heat and simmer gently for 15–20 minutes until the vegetables are tender. Remove from the heat and leave to cool for 30 minutes.

Heat the oil in a large, heavy-based frying pan. Add the onions and cook over a medium heat for about 2–3 minutes, stirring frequently, until golden brown. Remove the onions with a slotted spoon and drain well on absorbent kitchen paper. As they cool, they will turn crispy.

Pour the cooled soup into a food processor or blender and process to form a smooth purée. Return to the cleaned pan, adjust the seasoning, then stir in the cream. Gently reheat and top with the crispy onions. Serve immediately with chunks of bread.

Roasted Red Pepper, Tomato & Red Onion Soup

Serves 4

fine spray of oil
2 large red peppers, deseeded and
roughly chopped
1 red onion, peeled and
roughly chopped
350 g/12 oz tomatoes, halved
1 small crusty French loaf
1 garlic clove, peeled
600 ml/1 pint vegetable stock
salt and freshly ground
black pepper
1 tsp vegetarian Worcestershire
sauce
4 tbsp fromage frais

Preheat the oven to 190°C/375°F/Gas Mark 5. Spray a large roasting tin with the oil and place the peppers and onion in the base. Cook in the oven for 10 minutes. Add the tomatoes and cook for a further 20 minutes, or until the peppers are soft.

Cut the bread into 1 cm/1/2 inch slices. Cut the garlic clove in half and rub the cut edge of the garlic over the bread.

Place all the bread slices on a large baking tray, and bake in the preheated oven for 10 minutes, turning halfway through, until golden and crisp.

Remove the vegetables from the oven and allow to cool slightly, then blend in a food processor until smooth. Strain the vegetable mixture through a large nylon sieve into a saucepan, to remove the seeds and skin. Add the stock, season to taste with salt and pepper and stir to mix. Heat the soup gently until piping hot.

In a small bowl, beat together the Worcestershire sauce with the fromage frais.

Pour the soup into warm bowls and swirl a spoonful of the fromage frais mixture into each bowl. Serve immediately with the garlic toasts.

Carrot & Ginger Soup

Serves 4

4 slices bread, crusts removed
1 tsp yeast extract
2 tsp olive oil
1 onion, peeled and chopped
1 garlic clove, peeled and crushed
$1/2$ tsp ground ginger
450 g/1 lb carrots, peeled
and chopped
1 litre/$1^3/4$ pints vegetable stock
2.5 cm/1 inch piece root ginger,
peeled and finely grated
salt and freshly ground
black pepper
1 tbsp lemon juice

To garnish:

chives
lemon zest

Preheat the oven to 180°C/350°F/Gas Mark 4. Roughly chop the bread. Dissolve the yeast extract in 2 tablespoons of warm water and mix with the bread.

Spread the bread cubes over a lightly oiled baking tray and bake for 20 minutes, turning halfway through. Remove from the oven and reserve.

Heat the oil in a large saucepan. Gently cook the onion and garlic for 3–4 minutes.

Stir in the ground ginger and cook for 1 minute to release the flavour.

Add the chopped carrots, then stir in the stock and the fresh ginger. Simmer gently for 15 minutes.

Remove from the heat and allow to cool a little. Blend until smooth, then season to taste with salt and pepper. Stir in the lemon juice. Garnish with the chives and lemon zest and serve immediately.

Italian Bean Soup

Serves 4

2 tsp olive oil
1 leek, washed and chopped
1 garlic clove, peeled and crushed
2 tsp dried oregano
75 g/3 oz green beans, trimmed and
cut into bite-size pieces
410 g can cannellini beans,
drained and rinsed
75 g/3 oz small pasta shapes
1 litre/1³/₄ pints vegetable stock
8 cherry tomatoes
salt and freshly ground
black pepper
3 tbsp freshly shredded basil

Heat the oil in a large saucepan. Add the leek, garlic and oregano and cook gently for 5 minutes, stirring occasionally.

Stir in the green beans and the cannellini beans. Sprinkle in the pasta and pour in the stock.

Bring the stock mixture to the boil, then reduce the heat to a simmer.

Cook for 12–15 minutes until the vegetables are tender and the pasta is cooked *al dente*. Stir occasionally.

In a heavy-based frying pan, dry-fry the tomatoes over a high heat until they soften and the skins begin to blacken.

Gently crush the tomatoes in the pan with the back of a spoon and add to the soup.

Season to taste with salt and pepper. Stir in the shredded basil and serve immediately.

Tomato & Basil Soup

Serves 4

1.1 kg/2¹/₂ lb ripe tomatoes,
cut in half
2 garlic cloves
1 tsp olive oil
1 tbsp balsamic vinegar
1 tbsp dark brown sugar
1 tbsp tomato purée
300 ml/¹/₂ pint vegetable stock
6 tbsp natural yogurt
2 tbsp freshly chopped basil
salt and freshly ground
black pepper
small basil leaves, to garnish

Preheat the oven to 200°C/400°F/Gas Mark 6. Evenly spread the tomatoes and unpeeled garlic in a single layer in a large roasting tin.

Mix the oil and vinegar together. Drizzle over the tomatoes and sprinkle with the dark brown sugar.

Roast the tomatoes in the preheated oven for 20 minutes until tender and lightly charred in places.

Remove from the oven and allow to cool slightly. When cool enough to handle, squeeze the softened flesh of the garlic from the papery skin. Place with the charred tomatoes in a nylon sieve over a saucepan.

Press the garlic and tomatoes through the sieve with the back of a wooden spoon.

When all the flesh has been sieved, add the tomato purée and vegetable stock to the pan. Heat gently, stirring occasionally.

In a small bowl, beat the yogurt and basil together and season to taste with salt and pepper. Stir the basil yogurt into the soup. Garnish with basil leaves and serve immediately.

Curried Parsnip Soup

Serves 4

1 tsp cumin seeds
2 tsp coriander seeds
1 tsp oil
1 onion, peeled and chopped
1 garlic clove, peeled and crushed
$^1/_2$ tsp turmeric
$^1/_4$ tsp chilli powder
1 cinnamon stick
450 g/1 lb parsnips, peeled
and chopped
1 litre/1$^3/_4$ pints vegetable stock
salt and freshly ground
black pepper
fresh coriander leaves, to garnish
2–3 tbsp natural yogurt, to serve

In a small frying pan, dry-fry the cumin and coriander seeds over a moderately high heat for 1–2 minutes. Shake the pan during cooking until the seeds are lightly toasted.

Reserve until cooled. Grind the toasted seeds in a pestle and mortar.

Heat the oil in a saucepan. Cook the onion until softened and starting to turn golden.

Add the garlic, turmeric, chilli powder and cinnamon stick to the pan. Continue to cook for a further minute.

Add the parsnips and stir well. Pour in the stock and bring to the boil. Cover and simmer for 15 minutes, or until the parsnips are cooked.

Allow the soup to cool. Once cooled, remove the cinnamon stick and discard.

Blend the soup in a food processor until very smooth.

Transfer to a saucepan and reheat gently. Season to taste with salt and pepper. Garnish with fresh coriander and serve immediately with the yogurt.

Cream of Spinach Soup

Serves 6–8

1 large onion, peeled and chopped
5 large, plump garlic cloves, peeled and chopped
2 medium potatoes, peeled and chopped
750 ml/1¼ pints cold water
1 tsp salt
450 g/1 lb spinach, washed and large stems removed
50 g/2 oz butter
3 tbsp flour
750 ml/1¼ pints milk
½ tsp freshly grated nutmeg
freshly ground black pepper
6–8 tbsp crème fraîche or sour cream
warm focaccia bread, to serve

Place the onion, garlic and potatoes in a large saucepan and cover with the cold water. Add half the salt and bring to the boil. Cover and simmer for 15–20 minutes until the potatoes are tender. Remove from the heat and add the spinach. Cover and set aside for 10 minutes.

Slowly melt the butter in another saucepan, add the flour and cook over a low heat for about 2 minutes. Remove the saucepan from the heat and add the milk, a little at a time, stirring continuously. Return to the heat and cook, stirring continuously, for 5–8 minutes until the sauce is smooth and slightly thickened. Add the freshly grated nutmeg to taste.

Blend the cooled potato and spinach mixture in a food processor or blender to a smooth purée, then return to the saucepan and gradually stir in the white sauce. Season to taste with salt and pepper and gently reheat, taking care not to allow the soup to boil. Ladle into soup bowls and top with spoonfuls of crème fraîche or sour cream. Serve immediately with warm focaccia bread.

Hot & Sour Mushroom Soup

Serves 4

4 tbsp sunflower oil
3 garlic cloves, peeled and
finely chopped
3 shallots, peeled and
finely chopped
2 large red chillies, deseeded and
finely chopped
1 tbsp soft brown sugar
large pinch salt
1 litre/1³/₄ pints vegetable stock
250 g/9 oz Thai fragrant rice
5 kaffir lime leaves, torn
2 tbsp soy sauce
grated zest and juice of 1 lemon
250 g/9 oz oyster mushrooms, wiped
and cut into pieces
2 tbsp freshly chopped coriander

To garnish:

2 green chillies, deseeded and
finely chopped
3 spring onions, trimmed and
finely chopped

Heat the oil in a frying pan, add the garlic and shallots and cook until golden brown and starting to crisp. Remove from the pan and reserve. Add the chillies to the pan and cook until they start to change colour.

Place the garlic, shallots and chillies in a food processor or blender and blend to a smooth purée with 150 ml/¹/₄ pint water. Pour the purée back into the pan, add the sugar and the salt, then cook gently, stirring, until dark in colour. Take care not to burn the mixture.

Pour the stock into a large saucepan, add the garlic purée, rice, lime leaves, soy sauce and the lemon zest and juice. Bring to the boil, then reduce the heat, cover and simmer gently for about 10 minutes.

Add the mushrooms and simmer for a further 10 minutes, or until the mushrooms and rice are tender. Remove the lime leaves, stir in the chopped coriander and ladle into bowls. Place the chopped green chillies and spring onions in small bowls and serve separately to sprinkle on top of the soup.

Vegetable & Coconut Stew

Serves 4–6

2 tbsp vegetable oil or ghee
1 tsp cumin seeds
1 cinnamon stick, bruised
3 whole cloves
3 cardamom pods, bruised
$^1/_2$–1 tsp chilli powder
8 shallots, peeled and halved
2–3 garlic cloves, peeled and
finely chopped
225 g/8 oz potatoes, peeled and cut
into chunks
$^1/_2$ butternut squash, about 350 g/
12 oz in weight, peeled, deseeded
and cut into chunks
225 g/8 oz carrots, peeled and chopped
200 ml/7 fl oz water
300 ml/$^1/_2$ pint coconut milk
225 g/8 oz French beans, trimmed
and chopped
400 g/14 oz can red kidney beans,
drained and rinsed
4–6 spring onions, trimmed and
finely chopped

Heat the oil or ghee in a large saucepan, add the seeds, cinnamon stick, cloves, cardamom pods and chilli powder and fry for 30 seconds, or until the seeds pop.

Add the shallots, garlic, potatoes, squash and carrots and stir until the vegetables are coated in the flavoured oil. Add the water, bring to the boil, then reduce the heat, cover and simmer for 15 minutes.

Pour in the coconut milk and add the chopped beans and kidney beans. Stir well, then cook for a further 10 minutes. Sprinkle with the chopped spring onions and serve.

Black Bean Chilli with Avocado Salsa

Serves 4

250 g/9 oz black beans and black-eye
beans, soaked overnight
2 tbsp olive oil
1 onion, peeled and finely chopped
1 red pepper, deseeded and diced
2 garlic cloves, peeled and finely
chopped
1 red chilli, deseeded and finely
chopped
2 tsp chilli powder
1 tsp ground cumin
2 tsp ground coriander
400 g can chopped tomatoes
450 ml/³/₄ pint vegetable stock
1 small, ripe avocado, diced

¹/₂ small red onion, peeled and
finely chopped
2 tbsp freshly chopped coriander
juice of 1 lime
1 tomato, peeled, deseeded and diced
salt and freshly ground black pepper
25 g/1 oz dark chocolate
crème fraîche, lime slices and
coriander sprigs, to garnish

Drain the beans and place in a large saucepan with at least twice
their volume of fresh water. Bring slowly to the boil, skimming off
any froth. Boil rapidly for 10 minutes, then reduce the heat and
simmer for about 45 minutes, adding more water if necessary.
Drain and reserve.

Heat the oil in a large saucepan and add the onion and pepper.
Cook for 3–4 minutes until softened. Add the garlic and chilli. Cook
for 5 minutes, or until the onion and pepper have softened. Add
the chilli powder, cumin and coriander and cook for 30 seconds.
Add the beans along with the tomatoes and stock. Bring to the
boil and simmer uncovered for 40–45 minutes until the beans and
vegetables are tender and the sauce has reduced.

Mix together the avocado, onion, fresh coriander, lime juice and
tomato. Season with salt and pepper and reserve. Remove the
chilli from the heat. Break the chocolate into pieces. Sprinkle over
the chilli. Leave for 2 minutes. Stir well. Garnish with crème fraîche,
lime and coriander. Serve with the avocado salsa.

Mushroom Stew

Serves 4

15 g/¹/₂ oz dried porcini mushrooms
900 g/2 lb assorted fresh
mushrooms, wiped
2 tbsp good-quality virgin olive oil
1 onion, peeled and finely chopped
2 garlic cloves, peeled and
finely chopped
1 tbsp fresh thyme leaves
pinch ground cloves
salt and freshly ground black pepper
700 g/1¹/₂ lb tomatoes, peeled,
deseeded and chopped
225 g/8 oz instant polenta
600 ml/1 pint vegetable stock
3 tbsp freshly chopped mixed herbs
parsley sprigs, to garnish

Soak the porcini mushrooms in a small bowl of hot water for 20 minutes. Drain, reserving the mushrooms and their soaking liquid. Cut the fresh mushrooms in half and reserve.

In a saucepan, heat the oil and add the onion. Cook gently for 5–7 minutes until softened. Add the garlic, thyme and cloves and continue cooking for 2 minutes. Add all the mushrooms and cook for 8–10 minutes until the mushrooms have softened, stirring often. Season to taste with salt and pepper and add the tomatoes and the reserved soaking liquid. Simmer, partly covered, over a low heat for about 20 minutes until thickened. Adjust the seasoning to taste.

Meanwhile, cook the polenta according to the packet instructions using the vegetable stock. Stir in the herbs and divide between four dishes.

Ladle the mushrooms over the polenta, garnish with the parsley and serve immediately.

Pastas

Everyone loves pasta – it's one of the most delicious and simple foods to make! In this section, you will find classic recipes such as Pasta Primavera, but also vegetarian twists on everyone's culinary default. Revel in the tasty Rigatoni with Oven-dried Cherry Tomatoes & Mascarpone or delight in the taste of Pasta Shells with Broccoli & Capers.

Vegetarian Spaghetti Bolognese

Serves 4

2 tbsp olive oil
1 onion, peeled and finely chopped
1 carrot, peeled and
finely chopped
1 celery stalk, trimmed and
finely chopped
225 g/8 oz Quorn mince
150 ml/5 fl oz red wine
300 ml/¹/₂ pint vegetable stock
1 tsp mushroom ketchup
4 tbsp tomato purée
350 g/12 oz dried spaghetti
4 tbsp crème fraîche
salt and freshly ground
black pepper
1 tbsp freshly chopped parsley

Heat the oil in a large saucepan and add the onion, carrot and celery. Cook gently for 10 minutes, adding a little water if necessary, until softened and starting to brown.

Add the Quorn mince and cook for a further 2–3 minutes before adding the red wine. Increase the heat and simmer gently until nearly all the wine has evaporated.

Mix together the vegetable stock and mushroom ketchup and add about half to the Quorn mixture along with the tomato purée. Cover and simmer gently for about 45 minutes, adding the remaining stock as necessary.

Meanwhile, bring a large pan of salted water to the boil and add the spaghetti. Cook until *al dente*, or according to the packet instructions. Drain well. Remove the sauce from the heat, add the crème fraîche and season to taste with salt and pepper. Stir in the parsley and serve immediately with the pasta.

Tagliatelle with Broccoli & Sesame

Serves 2

225 g/8 oz broccoli, cut into florets
125 g/4 oz baby corn
175 g/6 oz dried tagliatelle
1¹/₂ tbsp tahini paste
1 tbsp dark soy sauce
1 tbsp dark muscovado sugar
1 tbsp red wine vinegar
1 tbsp sunflower oil
1 garlic clove, peeled and
finely chopped
2.5 cm/1 inch piece fresh root
ginger, peeled and shredded
¹/₂ tsp dried chilli flakes
salt and freshly ground
black pepper
1 tbsp toasted sesame seeds
radish slices, to garnish

Bring a large saucepan of salted water to the boil and add the broccoli and corn. Return the water to the boil, then remove the vegetables at once using a slotted spoon, reserving the water. Plunge them into cold water and drain well. Dry on kitchen paper and reserve.

Return the water to the boil. Add the tagliatelle and cook until *al dente* or according to the packet instructions. Drain well. Run under cold water until cold, then drain well again.

Place the tahini, soy sauce, sugar and vinegar into a bowl. Mix well, then reserve. Heat the oil in a wok or large frying pan over a high heat and add the garlic, ginger and chilli flakes and stir-fry for about 30 seconds. Add the broccoli and baby corn and continue to stir-fry for about 3 minutes.

Add the tagliatelle to the wok along with the tahini mixture and stir together for a further 1–2 minutes until heated through. Season to taste with salt and pepper. Sprinkle with sesame seeds, garnish with the radish slices and serve immediately.

Pasta Primavera

Serves 4

150 g/5 oz French beans
150 g/5 oz sugar snap peas
40 g/1½ oz butter
1 tsp olive oil
225 g/8 oz baby carrots, scrubbed
2 courgettes, trimmed
and thinly sliced
175 g/6 oz baby leeks, trimmed and
cut into 2.5 cm/1 inch lengths
200 ml/7 fl oz double cream
1 tsp finely grated lemon zest
350 g/12 oz dried tagliatelle
25 g/1 oz vegetarian Italian hard
cheese, grated
1 tbsp freshly snipped chives
1 tbsp freshly chopped dill
salt and freshly ground
black pepper
fresh dill sprigs, to garnish

Trim and halve the French beans. Bring a large saucepan of lightly salted water to the boil and cook the beans for 4–5 minutes, adding the sugar snap peas after 2 minutes, so that both are tender at the same time. Drain the beans and peas and briefly rinse under cold running water.

Heat the butter and oil in a large, nonstick frying pan. Add the baby carrots and cook for 2 minutes, then stir in the courgettes and leeks and cook for 10 minutes, stirring, until the vegetables are almost tender. Stir the cream and lemon zest into the vegetables and bubble over a gentle heat until the sauce is slightly reduced and the vegetables are cooked.

Meanwhile, bring a large saucepan of lightly salted water to the boil and cook the tagliatelle for 10 minutes, or until *al dente*.

Add the beans, sugar snaps, Italian hard cheese and herbs to the sauce. Stir for 30 seconds, or until the cheese has melted and the vegetables are hot.

Drain the tagliatelle, add the vegetables and sauce, then toss gently to mix and season to taste with salt and pepper. Spoon into a warm serving bowl, garnish with a few sprigs of dill and serve immediately.

Pasta Shells with Broccoli & Capers

Serves 4

400 g/14 oz conchiglie or orecchiette
(pasta shells)
450 g/1 lb broccoli florets, cut into
small pieces
5 tbsp olive oil
1 large onion, peeled and
finely chopped
4 tbsp capers in brine, rinsed
and drained
¹/₂ tsp dried chilli flakes (optional)
75 g/3 oz freshly grated vegetarian
Italian hard cheese, plus extra
to serve
25 g/1 oz vegetarian pecorino
cheese, grated
salt and freshly ground black pepper
2 tbsp freshly chopped flat-leaf
parsley, to garnish

Bring a large pan of lightly salted water to a rolling boil. Add the pasta shells, return to the boil and cook for 2 minutes. Add the broccoli to the pan. Return to the boil and continue cooking for 8–10 minutes until the pasta is *al dente*.

Meanwhile, heat the olive oil in a large frying pan, add the onion and cook for 5 minutes, or until softened, stirring frequently. Stir in the capers and chilli flakes, if using, and cook for a further 2 minutes.

Drain the pasta and broccoli and add to the frying pan. Toss the ingredients to mix thoroughly. Sprinkle over the cheeses, then stir until the cheeses have just melted. Season to taste with salt and pepper, then tip into a warm serving dish. Garnish with chopped parsley and serve immediately with extra Italian hard cheese.

Cannelloni with Tomato & Red Wine Sauce

Serves 6

2 tbsp olive oil
1 onion, peeled and finely chopped
1 garlic clove, peeled and crushed
250 g carton vegetarian
ricotta cheese
50 g/2 oz pine nuts
salt and freshly ground black pepper
pinch freshly grated nutmeg
250 g/9 oz fresh spinach lasagne
25 g/1 oz butter
1 shallot, peeled and finely chopped
150 ml/¼ pint red wine
400 g can chopped tomatoes
½ tsp sugar
50 g/2 oz vegetarian mozzarella
cheese, grated, plus extra to serve
1 tbsp freshly chopped parsley,
to garnish
fresh green salad, to serve

Preheat the oven to 200°C/400°F/Gas Mark 6, 15 minutes before cooking. Heat the oil in a heavy-based pan, add the onion and garlic and cook for 2–3 minutes. Cool slightly, then stir in the ricotta cheese and pine nuts. Season the filling to taste with salt, pepper and the nutmeg.

Cut each lasagne sheet in half, put a little of the ricotta filling on each piece and roll up like a cigar to resemble cannelloni tubes. Arrange the cannelloni, seam-side down, in a single layer, in a lightly oiled, 2.3 litre/4 pint shallow, ovenproof dish.

Melt the butter in a pan, add the shallot and cook for 2 minutes. Pour in the red wine, tomatoes and sugar and season well. Bring to the boil, lower the heat and simmer for about 20 minutes until thickened. Add a little more sugar if desired. Transfer to a food processor and blend until a smooth sauce is formed.

Pour the warm tomato sauce over the cannelloni and sprinkle with the grated vegetarian vegetarian mozzarella cheese. Bake in the preheated oven for about 30 minutes until golden and bubbling. Garnish with parsley and serve immediately with a green salad.

Spaghettini with Lemon Pesto & Cheese & Herb Bread

Serves 6

1 small onion, peeled and grated
2 tsp freshly chopped oregano
1 tbsp freshly chopped parsley
75 g/3 oz butter
125 g/4 oz vegetarian pecorino
cheese, grated
8 slices Italian flatbread
275 g/10 oz dried spaghettini
4 tbsp olive oil
1 large bunch basil,
approximately 25 g/1 oz
75 g/3 oz pine nuts
1 garlic clove, peeled and crushed
75 g/3 oz vegetarian Italian hard
cheese, grated
finely grated zest and juice
of 2 lemons
salt and freshly ground black pepper
4 tsp butter

Preheat the oven to 200°C/400°F/Gas Mark 6, 15 minutes before baking. Mix together the onion, oregano, parsley, butter and cheese. Spread the bread with the cheese mixture, place on a lightly oiled baking tray and cover with kitchen foil. Bake in the preheated oven for 10–15 minutes, then keep warm.

Add the spaghettini with 1 tablespoon olive oil to a large saucepan of fast-boiling, lightly salted water and cook for 3–4 minutes, or until *al dente*. Drain, reserving 2 tablespoons of the cooking liquor.

Blend the basil, pine nuts, garlic, Italian hard cheese, lemon zest and juice and remaining olive oil in a food processor or blender until a purée is formed. Season to taste with salt and pepper, then place in a saucepan. Heat the lemon pesto very gently until piping hot, then stir in the pasta together with the reserved cooking liquor. Add the butter and mix well together.

Add plenty of black pepper to the pasta and serve immediately with the warm cheese and herb bread.

Courgette Lasagne

Serves 8

2 tbsp olive oil

1 medium onion, peeled and finely chopped

225 g/8 oz mushrooms, wiped and thinly sliced

3–4 courgettes, trimmed and thinly sliced

2 garlic cloves, peeled and finely chopped

$^1/_2$ tsp dried thyme

1–2 tbsp freshly chopped basil or flat-leaf parsley

salt and freshly ground black pepper

75 g/3 oz butter

4 tbsp plain flour

750 ml/1$^1/_4$ pints milk

$^1/_4$ tsp freshly ground nutmeg

350 g/12 oz lasagne sheets, cooked

225 g/8 oz vegetarian mozzarella cheese, grated

50 g/2 oz vegetarian Italian hard cheese, grated

400 g can chopped tomatoes, drained

Preheat the oven to 200°C/400°F/Gas Mark 6, 15 minutes before cooking. Heat the oil in a large frying pan, add the onion and cook for 3–5 minutes. Add the mushrooms, cook for 2 minutes, then add the courgettes and cook for a further 3–4 minutes until tender. Stir in the garlic, thyme and basil or parsley and season to taste with salt and pepper. Remove from the heat and reserve.

Melt the butter in a small heavy-based pan, add the flour and cook gently, stirring, for 2 minutes. Remove from the heat and gradually stir in the milk. Return to the heat and cook, stirring, for 2 minutes, or until the sauce thickens. Bring to the boil, remove from the heat and stir in the mustard. Season to taste with salt, pepper and nutmeg. Spoon one third of the white sauce onto the base of a lightly oiled, large baking dish. Arrange a layer of lasagne over the sauce. Spread half the courgette mixture over the pasta, then sprinkle with some of the vegetarian mozzarella and some of the Italian hard cheese. Repeat with more white sauce and another layer of lasagne, then cover with half the drained tomatoes.

Cover the tomatoes with lasagne, the remaining courgette mixture and some vegetarian mozzarella and Italian hard cheese. Repeat the layers, ending with a layer of lasagne sheets, white sauce and the remaining Italian hard cheese. Bake in the preheated oven for 35 minutes, or until golden. Serve immediately.

Spinach & Ricotta Gnocchi with Butter & Italian Hard Cheese

Serves 2–4

125 g/4 oz frozen leaf spinach, thawed
225 g/8 oz vegetarian ricotta cheese
50 g/2 oz freshly grated vegetarian
Italian hard cheese
2 small eggs, lightly beaten
salt and freshly ground black pepper
2 tbsp freshly chopped basil
50 g/2 oz plain flour
50 g/2 oz unsalted butter
2 garlic cloves, peeled and crushed
vegetarian Italian hard cheese
shavings, to serve

Squeeze the excess moisture from the spinach and chop finely. Blend in a food processor with the ricotta cheese, Italian hard cheese, eggs, seasoning and 1 tablespoon of the basil until smooth. Scrape into a bowl, then add sufficient flour to form a soft, slightly sticky dough.

Bring a large pan of salted water to a rolling boil. Transfer the spinach mixture to a piping bag fitted with a large plain nozzle. As soon as the water is boiling, pipe 10–12 short lengths of the mixture into the water, using a sharp knife to cut the gnocchi as you go.

Bring the water back to the boil and cook the gnocchi for 3–4 minutes until they begin to rise to the surface. Remove with a slotted spoon, drain on absorbent kitchen paper and transfer to a warm serving dish. Cook the gnocchi in batches if necessary.

Melt the butter in a small frying pan and, when foaming, add the garlic and remaining basil. Remove from the heat and immediately pour over the cooked gnocchi. Season well with salt and pepper and serve immediately with extra grated Italian hard cheese.

Spaghettini with Peas, Spring Onions & Mint

Serves 6

pinch saffron strands
700 g/1¹/₂ lb fresh peas or 350 g/
12 oz frozen petit pois, thawed
75 g/3 oz unsalted butter, softened
6 spring onions, trimmed and
finely sliced
salt and freshly ground black pepper
1 garlic clove, peeled and
finely chopped
2 tbsp freshly chopped mint
450 g/1 lb spaghettini
freshly grated vegetarian Italian hard
cheese, to serve

Soak the saffron in 2 tablespoons hot water while you prepare the sauce. Shell the peas if using fresh ones.

Heat 50 g/2 oz of the butter in a medium frying pan, add the spring onions and a little salt and cook over a low heat for 2–3 minutes until the onions are softened. Add the garlic, then the peas and 100 ml/3¹/₂ fl oz water. Bring to the boil and cook for 5–6 minutes until the peas are just tender. Stir in the mint and keep warm.

Blend the remaining butter and the saffron water in a large, warm serving bowl and reserve.

Meanwhile, bring a large pan of lightly salted water to a rolling boil and add the spaghettini. Cook according to the packet instructions, or until *al dente*.

Drain thoroughly, reserving 2–3 tablespoons of the pasta cooking water. Tip into a warm serving bowl, add the pea sauce and toss together gently. Season to taste with salt and pepper. Serve immediately with extra black pepper and grated Italian hard cheese.

Aubergine & Ravioli Parmigiana

Serves 6

4 tbsp olive oil
1 large onion, peeled and
finely chopped
2–3 garlic cloves, peeled
and crushed
2 x 400 g cans chopped tomatoes
2 tsp brown sugar
1 dried bay leaf
1 tsp dried oregano
1 tsp dried basil
2 tbsp freshly shredded basil
salt and freshly ground black pepper
2–3 medium aubergines, sliced
crossways 1 cm/¹/₂ inch thick
2 medium eggs, beaten with
1 tbsp water
125 g/4 oz dried breadcrumbs
75 g/3 oz freshly grated vegetarian
Italian hard cheese
400 g/14 oz vegetarian mozzarella
cheese, thinly sliced
250 g/9 oz cheese-filled ravioli,
cooked and drained

Preheat the oven to 180°C/350°F/Gas Mark 4, about 15 minutes before cooking. Heat 2 tablespoons of the olive oil in a large, heavy-based pan, add the onion and cook for 6–7 minutes until softened. Add the garlic, cook for 1 minute, then stir in the tomatoes, sugar, bay leaf, dried oregano and basil, then bring to the boil, stirring frequently. Simmer for 30–35 minutes until thickened and reduced, stirring occasionally. Stir in the fresh basil and season to taste with salt and pepper. Remove the tomato sauce from the heat and reserve.

Heat the remaining olive oil in a large, heavy-based frying pan over a high heat. Dip the aubergine slices in the egg mixture, then in the breadcrumbs. Cook in batches until golden on both sides. Drain on absorbent kitchen paper. Add more oil between batches if necessary.

Spoon a little tomato sauce into the base of a lightly oiled, large baking dish. Cover with a layer of aubergine slices, a sprinkling of Italian hard cheese, a layer of vegetarian mozzarella cheese, then more sauce. Repeat the layers, then cover the sauce with a layer of cooked ravioli. Continue to layer in this way, ending with a layer of mozzarella cheese. Sprinkle the top with Italian hard cheese. Drizzle with a little extra olive oil if liked, then bake in the preheated oven for 30 minutes, or until golden-brown and bubbling. Serve immediately.

Rigatoni with Oven-dried Cherry Tomatoes & Mascarpone

Serves 4

350 g/12 oz red cherry tomatoes
1 tsp caster sugar
salt and freshly ground
black pepper
2 tbsp olive oil
400 g/14 oz dried rigatoni
125 g/4 oz petits pois
2 tbsp mascarpone cheese
1 tbsp freshly chopped mint
1 tbsp freshly chopped parsley
sprigs of fresh mint, to garnish

Preheat oven to 140°C/ 275°F/Gas Mark 1. Halve the cherry tomatoes and place close together on a non-stick baking tray, cut-side up. Sprinkle lightly with the sugar, then with a little salt and pepper. Bake in the preheated oven for 1¼ hours, or until dry, but not beginning to colour. Leave to cool on the baking tray. Put in a bowl, drizzle over the olive oil and toss to coat.

Bring a large saucepan of lightly salted water to the boil and cook the pasta for about 10 minutes or until 'al dente'. Add the petits pois, 2–3 minutes before the end of the cooking time. Drain thoroughly and return the pasta and the petits pois to the saucepan.

Add the mascarpone to the saucepan. When melted, add the tomatoes, mint, parsley and a little black pepper. Toss gently together, then transfer to a warmed serving dish or individual plates and garnish with sprigs of fresh mint. Serve immediately.

Baked Macaroni with Mushrooms & Leeks

Serves 4

2 tbsp olive oil
1 onion, peeled and finely chopped
1 garlic clove, peeled and crushed
2 small leeks, trimmed and chopped
450 g/1 lb assorted wild
mushrooms, trimmed
75 g/3 oz butter
50 ml/2 fl oz white wine
150 ml/¹/₄ pint crème fraîche or
whipping cream
salt and freshly ground black pepper
350 g/12 oz short cut macaroni
75 g/3 oz fresh white breadcrumbs
1 tbsp freshly chopped parsley,
to garnish

Preheat the oven to 220°C/425°F/Gas Mark 7, 15 minutes before cooking. Heat 1 tablespoon of the olive oil in a large frying pan, add the onion and garlic and cook for 2 minutes. Add the leeks, mushrooms and 25 g/1 oz of the butter, then cook for 5 minutes. Pour in the white wine, cook for 2 minutes, then stir in the crème fraîche or cream. Season to taste with salt and pepper.

Meanwhile, bring a large pan of lightly salted water to a rolling boil. Add the macaroni and cook according to the packet instructions, or until *al dente*.

Melt 25 g/1 oz of the butter with the remaining oil in a small frying pan. Add the breadcrumbs and fry until just beginning to turn golden brown. Drain on absorbent kitchen paper.

Drain the pasta thoroughly, toss in the remaining butter, then tip into a lightly oiled 1.4 litre/2¹/₂ pint shallow baking dish. Cover the pasta with the leek and mushroom mixture, then sprinkle with the fried breadcrumbs. Bake in the preheated oven for 5–10 minutes until golden and crisp. Garnish with chopped parsley and serve.

Tagliarini with Broad Beans, Saffron & Crème Fraîche

Serves 2–3

225 g/8 oz fresh young broad beans
in pods, or 100 g/3¹/₂ oz frozen
broad beans, thawed
1 tbsp olive oil
1 garlic clove, peeled and chopped
small handful basil leaves, shredded
200 ml/7 fl oz crème fraîche
large pinch saffron strands
350 g/12 oz tagliarini
salt and freshly ground black pepper
1 tbsp freshly snipped chives
freshly grated vegetarian Italian hard
cheese, to serve

If using fresh broad beans, bring a pan of lightly salted water to the boil. Pod the beans and drop them into the boiling water for 1 minute. Drain and refresh under cold water. Drain again. Remove the outer skins of the beans and discard. If using thawed frozen broad beans, remove and discard the skins. Reserve the peeled beans.

Heat the olive oil in a saucepan. Add the peeled broad beans and the garlic and cook gently for 2–3 minutes. Stir in the basil, the crème fraîche and the saffron strands and simmer for 1 minute.

Meanwhile, bring a large pan of lightly salted water to a rolling boil. Add the pasta and cook according to the packet instructions, or until *al dente*. Drain the pasta well and add to the sauce. Toss together and season to taste with salt and pepper.

Transfer the pasta and sauce to a warm serving dish. Sprinkle with snipped chives and serve immediately with grated Italian hard cheese.

Pies & Pastries

Savoury pies are a dinner choice that is often forgotten about, but the recipes in this section are sure to stick in your memory. To warm up on a cold night, enjoy the Roasted Vegetable Pie, or if you're having friends over, impress them with a gorgeous Parsnip Tatin!

Garlic Wild Mushroom Galettes

Serves 6

1 quantity quick flaky pastry
(*see* page 162), chilled
1 onion, peeled
1 red chilli, deseeded
2 garlic cloves, peeled
275 g/10 oz mixed mushrooms e.g.
oyster, chestnuts, morels,
ceps and chanterelles
25 g/1 oz butter
2 tbsp freshly chopped parsley
125 g/4 oz mozzarella
cheese, sliced

To serve:

cherry tomatoes
mixed green salad leaves

Preheat the oven to 220°C/425°F/Gas Mark 7. On a lightly floured surface, roll out the chilled pastry very thinly. Cut out six 15 cm/6 inch circles and place on a lightly oiled baking sheet.

Thinly slice the onion, then divide into rings and reserve.

Thinly slice the chilli and slice the garlic into wafer-thin slivers. Add to the onion and reserve.

Wipe or lightly rinse the mushrooms. Halve or quarter any large mushrooms and keep the small ones whole.

Heat the butter in a frying pan and sauté the onion, chilli and garlic gently for about 3 minutes. Add the mushrooms and cook for about 5 minutes until beginning to soften. Stir the parsley into the mushroom mixture and drain off any excess liquid.

Pile the mushroom mixture onto the pastry circles within 5 mm/1/4 inch of the edge. Arrange the sliced mozzarella cheese on top. Bake in the preheated oven for 12–15 minutes until golden brown and serve with the tomatoes and salad.

Potato & Goats' Cheese Tart

Serves 6

275 g/10 oz prepared shortcrust
pastry, thawed if frozen
550 g/1 lb 3 oz small waxy potatoes
beaten egg, for brushing
2 tbsp sun-dried tomato paste
¹/₄ tsp chilli powder, or to taste
1 large egg
150 ml/¹/₄ pint sour cream
150 ml/¹/₄ pint milk
2 tbsp freshly snipped chives
salt and freshly ground
black pepper
300 g/11 oz vegetarian
goats'cheese, sliced
salad and warm crusty bread,
to serve

Preheat the oven to 190°C/375°F/Gas Mark 5, about 10 minutes before cooking. Roll the pastry out on a lightly floured surface and use to line a 23 cm/9 inch fluted flan tin. Chill in the refrigerator for 30 minutes.

Scrub the potatoes, place in a large saucepan of lightly salted water and bring to the boil. Simmer for 10–15 minutes until the potatoes are tender. Drain and reserve.

Line the pastry case with greaseproof paper and baking beans or crumpled kitchen foil and bake blind in the preheated oven for 15 minutes. Remove from the oven and discard the paper and beans or foil. Brush the base with a little beaten egg, then return to the oven and cook for a further 5 minutes. Remove from the oven.

When the potatoes are cool enough to handle, cut into 1 cm/¹/₂ inch thick slices; reserve. Spread the sun-dried tomato paste over the base of the pastry case, sprinkle with the chilli powder, then arrange the potato slices on top in a decorative pattern.

Beat together the egg, sour cream, milk and chives, then season to taste with salt and pepper. Pour over the potatoes. Arrange the goats' cheese on top of the potatoes. Bake in the preheated oven for 30 minutes until golden brown and set. Serve immediately with salad and warm bread.

Stilton, Tomato & Courgette Quiche

Serves 4

For the shortcrust pastry:

150 g/5 oz plain flour
pinch salt
25 g/1 oz white vegetable fat,
cut into small cubes
40 g/1½ oz butter or hard block
margarine, cut into cubes

For the filling:

25 g/1 oz butter
1 onion, peeled and finely chopped
1 courgette, trimmed and sliced
125 g/4 oz vegetarian Stilton
cheese, crumbled
6 cherry tomatoes, halved
2 large eggs, beaten
200 ml tub crème fraîche
salt and freshly ground
black pepper

Sift the flour and salt into a large bowl. Add the fats and mix lightly. Using the fingertips, rub into the flour until the mixture resembles breadcrumbs. Sprinkle 1 tablespoon cold water into the mixture and, with a knife, start bringing the dough together. (It may be necessary to use the hands for the final stage.) If the dough does not form a ball instantly, add a little more water. Put the pastry in a polythene bag and chill for at least 30 minutes.

Preheat the oven to 190°C/375°F/Gas Mark 5. On a lightly floured surface, roll out the pastry and use to line an 18 cm/7 inch lightly oiled quiche or flan tin, trimming any excess pastry with a knife. Prick the base all over with a fork and bake blind in the preheated oven for 15 minutes. Remove the pastry from the oven and brush with a little of the beaten egg. Return to the oven for a further 5 minutes.

Heat the butter in a frying pan and gently fry the onion and courgette for about 4 minutes until soft and starting to brown. Transfer into the pastry case. Sprinkle the Stilton over evenly and top with the halved cherry tomatoes. Beat together the eggs and crème fraîche and season to taste with salt and pepper. Pour into the pastry case and bake in the oven for 35–40 minutes until the filling is golden brown and set in the centre. Serve the quiche hot or cold.

French Onion Tart

Serves 4

For the quick flaky pastry:

125 g/4 oz butter
175 g/6 oz plain flour
pinch salt

For the filling:

2 tbsp olive oil
4 large onions, peeled and
thinly sliced
3 tbsp white wine vinegar
2 tbsp muscovado sugar
175 g/6 oz vegetarian cheddar
cheese, grated
a little beaten egg or milk
salt and freshly ground
black pepper

Preheat the oven to 200°C/400°F/Gas Mark 6. Place the butter in the freezer for 30 minutes. Sift the flour and salt into a large bowl. Remove the butter from the freezer and grate using the coarse side of a grater, dipping the butter in the flour every now and again, as it makes it easier to grate. Mix the butter into the flour using a knife, making sure all the butter is coated thoroughly with flour. Add 2 tablespoons cold water and continue to mix, bringing the mixture together. Use your hands to complete the mixing. Add a little more water if needed, to leave a clean bowl. Place the pastry in a polythene bag and chill in the refrigerator for 30 minutes.

Heat the oil in a large frying pan, then fry the onions for 10 minutes, stirring occasionally, until softened. Stir in the white wine vinegar and sugar. Increase the heat and stir frequently for another 4–5 minutes until the onions turn a deep caramel colour. Cook for another 5 minutes, then reserve to cool.

On a lightly floured surface, roll out the pastry to a 35.5 cm/14 inch circle. Wrap over a rolling pin and move the circle onto a baking sheet. Sprinkle half the cheese over the pastry, leaving a 5 cm/2 inch border around the edge, then spoon the caramelised onions over the cheese. Fold the uncovered pastry edges over the edge of the filling to form a rim and brush the rim with beaten egg or milk. Season to taste with salt and pepper. Sprinkle over the remaining Cheddar and bake for 20–25 minutes. Transfer to a large plate and serve immediately.

Red Pepper & Basil Tart

Serves 4–6

For the olive pastry:

225 g/8 oz plain flour
pinch salt
1 medium egg, lightly beaten,
plus 1 egg yolk
3 tbsp olive oil
50 g/2 oz pitted black olives,
finely chopped

For the filling:

2 large red peppers, quartered
and deseeded
175 g/6 oz mascarpone cheese
4 tbsp milk
2 medium eggs
3 tbsp freshly chopped basil
salt and freshly ground
black pepper
fresh basil sprig, to garnish
mixed salad, to serve

Preheat the oven to 200°C/400°F/Gas Mark 6, 15 minutes before cooking. Sift the flour and salt into a bowl. Make a well in the centre. Stir together the egg, oil and 1 tablespoon of tepid water. Add to the dry ingredients, drop in the olives and mix to a dough. Knead on a lightly floured surface for a few seconds until smooth, then wrap in clingfilm and chill in the refrigerator for 30 minutes. Roll out the pastry and use to line a 23 cm/ 9 inch loose-bottomed, fluted flan tin. Lightly prick the base with a fork. Cover and chill in the refrigerator for 20 minutes.

Cook the peppers under a hot grill for 10 minutes, or until the skins are blackened and blistered. Put the peppers in a plastic bag, cool for 10 minutes, then remove the skins and slice.

Line the pastry case with kitchen foil or greaseproof paper weighed down with baking beans and bake in the preheated oven for 10 minutes. Remove the foil or greaseproof paper and beans and bake for a further 5 minutes. Reduce the oven temperature to 180°C/350°F/Gas Mark 4.

Beat the mascarpone cheese until smooth. Gradually add the milk and eggs. Stir in the peppers and basil and season to taste with salt and pepper. Spoon into the flan case and bake for 25–30 minutes until lightly set. Garnish with a sprig of fresh basil and serve immediately with a mixed salad.

Roasted Vegetable Pie

Serves 4

225 g/8 oz plain flour
pinch salt
50 g/2 oz white vegetable fat,
cut into squares
50 g/2 oz butter, cut into squares
2 tsp herbes de Provence
1 red pepper, deseeded and halved
1 green pepper, deseeded
and halved
1 yellow pepper, deseeded
and halved
3 tbsp extra virgin olive oil
1 aubergine, trimmed and sliced
1 courgette, trimmed and
halved lengthways
1 leek, trimmed and
cut into chunks
1 medium egg, beaten
125 g/4 oz fresh vegetarian
mozzarella cheese, sliced
salt and freshly ground
black pepper
mixed herb sprigs, to garnish

Preheat the oven to 220°C/425°F/Gas Mark 7. Sift the flour and salt into a large bowl, add the fats and mix lightly. Using the fingertips, rub into the flour until the mixture resembles breadcrumbs. Stir in the herbes de Provence. Sprinkle over a tablespoon cold water and, with a knife, start bringing the dough together (use your hands if necessary). If it does not form a ball instantly, add a little more water. Wrap in clingfilm and chill for 30 minutes. Whilst the pastry is chilling, place the peppers on a baking tray and sprinkle with 1 tablespoon of oil. Roast for 20 minutes, or until the skins start to blacken. Brush the aubergine, courgette and leek with oil and place on another tray. Roast with the peppers for 20 minutes. Place the peppers in a polythene bag and leave the skins to loosen for 5 minutes. When cool enough to handle, peel off the skins.

Roll out half the pastry on a floured surface and use to line a 20.5 cm/8 inch round pie dish. Line with greaseproof paper and fill with baking beans or rice and bake blind for about 10 minutes. Remove the beans and the paper, then brush the base with a little of the beaten egg. Return to the oven for 5 minutes. Layer the vegetables and the cheese in the pastry case, seasoning each layer. Roll out the remaining pastry on a floured surface and cut out a lid 5 mm/1⁄4 inch wider than the dish. Brush the rim with the egg, lay the lid on top and press to seal. Cut a slit in the lid and brush with the beaten egg. Bake for 30 minutes. Transfer to a serving dish, garnish with sprigs of mixed herbs and serve immediately.

Tomato & Courgette Herb Tart

Serves 4

4 tbsp olive oil
1 onion, peeled and finely chopped
3 garlic cloves, peeled and crushed
400 g/14 oz prepared puff pastry,
thawed if frozen
1 small egg, beaten
2 tbsp freshly chopped rosemary
2 tbsp freshly chopped parsley
175 g/6 oz rindless fresh soft
vegetarian goats' cheese
4 ripe plum tomatoes, sliced
1 medium courgette, trimmed
and sliced
thyme sprigs, to garnish

Preheat the oven to 230°C/450°F/Gas Mark 8. Heat 2 tablespoons of the oil in a large frying pan. Fry the onion and garlic for about 4 minutes until softened and reserve.

Roll out the pastry on a lightly floured surface and cut out a 30.5 cm/ 12 inch circle. Brush the pastry with a little beaten egg, then prick all over with a fork. Transfer onto a dampened baking sheet and bake in the preheated oven for 10 minutes. Turn the pastry over and brush with a little more egg. Bake for 5 more minutes, then remove from the oven.

Mix together the onion, garlic and herbs with the goats' cheese and spread over the pastry. Arrange the tomatoes and courgette over the goats' cheese and drizzle with the remaining oil. Bake for 20–25 minutes until the pastry is golden brown and the topping bubbling. Garnish with the thyme sprigs and serve immediately.

Leek & Potato Tart

Serves 6

225 g/8 oz plain flour
pinch salt
150 g/5 oz butter, cubed
50 g/2 oz walnuts, very
finely chopped
1 large egg yolk

For the filling:

450 g/1 lb leeks, trimmed and
thinly sliced
40 g/1½ oz butter
450 g/1 lb large new potatoes,
scrubbed
300 ml/½ pint sour cream
3 medium eggs, lightly beaten
175 g/6 oz vegetarian Gruyère
cheese, grated
freshly grated nutmeg
salt and freshly ground
black pepper
fresh chives, to garnish

Preheat the oven to 200°C/400°F/Gas Mark 6, about 15 minutes before baking. Sift the flour and salt into a bowl. Rub in the butter until the mixture resembles breadcrumbs. Stir in the nuts. Mix together the egg yolk and 3 tablespoons cold water. Sprinkle over the dry ingredients. Mix to form a dough.

Knead on a lightly floured surface for a few seconds, then wrap in clingfilm and chill in the refrigerator for 20 minutes. Roll out and use to line a 20.5 cm/8 inch springform tin or very deep flan tin. Chill for a further 30 minutes.

Cook the leeks in the butter over a high heat for 2–3 minutes, stirring constantly. Lower the heat, cover and cook for 25 minutes until soft, stirring occasionally. Remove the leeks from the heat.

Cook the potatoes in boiling salted water for 15 minutes, or until almost tender. Drain and thickly slice. Add to the leeks. Stir the sour cream into the leeks and potatoes, followed by the eggs, cheese, nutmeg, salt and pepper. Pour into the pastry case and bake on the middle shelf in the preheated oven for 20 minutes.

Reduce the oven temperature to 190°C/375°F/Gas Mark 5 and cook for a further 30–35 minutes until the filling is set. Garnish with chives and serve immediately.

Spinach, Pine Nut & Mascarpone Pizza

Serves 2–4

For the basic pizza dough:

225 g/8 oz strong plain flour
$^{1}/_{2}$ tsp salt
¼ tsp quick-acting dried yeast
150 ml/$^{1}/_{4}$ pint warm water
1 tbsp extra virgin olive oil

For the topping:

3 tbsp olive oil
1 large red onion, peeled
and chopped
2 garlic cloves, peeled
and finely sliced
450 g/1 lb frozen spinach, thawed
and drained
salt and freshly ground
black pepper
3 tbsp passata
125 g/4 oz mascarpone cheese
1 tbsp toasted pine nuts

Preheat the oven to 220°C/425°F/Gas Mark 7. Sift the flour and salt into a bowl and stir in the yeast. Make a well in the centre and gradually add the water and oil to form a soft dough. Knead the dough on a floured surface for about 5 minutes until smooth and elastic. Place in a lightly oiled bowl and cover with clingfilm. Leave to rise in a warm place for 1 hour.

Knock the pizza dough with your fist a few times, shape and roll out thinly on a lightly floured board. Place on a lightly floured baking sheet and lift the edge to make a little rim. Place another baking sheet into the preheated oven to heat up.

Heat half the oil in a frying pan and gently fry the onion and garlic until soft and starting to change colour.

Squeeze out any excess water from the spinach and finely chop. Add to the onion and garlic with the remaining olive oil. Season to taste with salt and pepper.

Spread the passata on the pizza dough and top with the spinach mixture. Mix the mascarpone with the pine nuts and dot over the pizza. Slide the pizza onto the hot baking sheet and bake for 15–20 minutes. Transfer to a large plate and serve immediately.

Chargrilled Vegetable & Goats' Cheese Pizza

Serves 4

125 g/4 oz baking potato
1 tbsp olive oil
225 g/8 oz strong white flour
1/2 tsp salt
1 tsp easy-blend dried yeast

For the topping:

1 medium aubergine, thinly sliced
2 small courgettes, trimmed and
sliced lengthways
1 yellow pepper, quartered and
deseeded
1 red onion, peeled and sliced into
very thin wedges
5 tbsp olive oil
175 g/6 oz cooked new
potatoes, halved
400 g can chopped tomatoes, drained
2 tsp freshly chopped oregano
125 g/4 oz vegetarian mozzarella
cheese, cut into small cubes
125 g/4 oz vegetarian goats'
cheese, crumbled

Preheat the oven to 220°C/425°F/Gas Mark 7, 15 minutes before baking. Put a baking sheet in the oven to heat up. Cook the potato in lightly salted boiling water until tender. Peel and mash with the olive oil until smooth.

Sift the flour and salt into a bowl. Stir in the yeast. Add the mashed potato and 150 ml/1/4 pint warm water and mix to a soft dough. Knead for 5–6 minutes until smooth. Put the dough in a bowl, cover with clingfilm and leave to rise in a warm place for 30 minutes.

To make the topping, arrange the aubergine, courgettes, pepper and onion, skin-side up, on a grill rack and brush with 4 tablespoons of the oil. Grill for 4–5 minutes. Turn the vegetables and brush with the remaining oil. Grill for 3–4 minutes. Cool, skin and slice the pepper. Put all of the vegetables in a bowl, add the halved new potatoes and toss gently together. Reserve.

Briefly re-knead the dough, then roll out to a 30.5–35.5 cm/12–14 inch round, according to preferred thickness. Mix the tomatoes and oregano together and spread over the pizza base. Scatter over the mozzarella cheese. Put the pizza on the preheated baking sheet and bake for 8 minutes. Arrange the vegetables and goats' cheese on top and bake for 8–10 minutes. Serve.

Cheese & Onion Oat Pie

Serves 4

1 tbsp sunflower oil,
plus 1 tsp
25 g/1 oz butter
2 medium onions, peeled
and sliced
1 garlic clove, peeled and crushed
150 g/5 oz porridge oats
125 g/4 oz mature vegetarian
cheddar cheese, grated
2 medium eggs, lightly beaten
2 tbsp freshly chopped parsley
salt and freshly ground
black pepper
275 g/10 oz baking potato, peeled

Preheat the oven to 180°C/350°F/Gas Mark 4. Heat the oil and half the butter in a saucepan until melted. Add the onions and garlic and gently cook for 10 minutes, or until soft. Remove from the heat and tip into a large bowl.

Spread the oats out on a baking sheet and toast in the hot oven for 12 minutes. Leave to cool, then add to the onions with the cheese, eggs and parsley. Season to taste with salt and pepper and mix well.

Line the base of a 20.5 cm/8 inch round sandwich tin with greaseproof paper and oil well. Thinly slice the potato and arrange the slices on the base, overlapping them slightly.

Spoon the cheese and oat mixture on top of the potato, spreading evenly with the back of a spoon. Cover with kitchen foil and bake for 30 minutes.

Invert the pie onto a baking sheet so that the potatoes are on top. Carefully remove the tin and lining paper. Preheat the grill to medium. Melt the remaining butter and carefully brush over the potato topping. Cook under the preheated grill for 5–6 minutes until the potatoes are lightly browned. Cut into wedges and serve.

Parsnip Tatin

Serves 4

1 quantity shortcrust pastry
(*see* page 160)

For the filling:

50 g/2 oz butter
8 small parsnips, peeled
and halved
1 tbsp brown sugar
85 ml/3 fl oz apple juice

Preheat the oven to 200°C/400°F/Gas Mark 6. Heat the butter in a
20.5 cm/8 inch frying pan.

Add the parsnips, arranging them cut-side down with the narrow ends
towards the centre. Sprinkle with sugar and cook for 15 minutes, turning
halfway through, until golden.

Add the apple juice and bring to the boil. Remove the pan from
the heat.

On a lightly floured surface, roll the pastry out to a size slightly larger
than the frying pan. Position the pastry over the parsnips and press
down slightly to enclose the parsnips. Bake in the preheated oven for
20–25 minutes until the parsnips and pastry are golden.

Invert a warm serving plate over the pan and carefully turn the pan over
to flip the tart onto the plate. Serve immediately.

Rice
Dishes

Tired of using rice purely as a base for curries and chilli? In this section, rice is not just a side; it's the star. Innovative recipes such as Wild Rice Dolmades and Rice Nuggets in Herby Tomato Sauce will have you thinking of rice in an all-new way!

Spring Vegetable & Herb Risotto

Serves 2–3

1 litre/1³/₄ pints vegetable stock
125 g/4 oz asparagus tips, trimmed
125 g/4 oz baby carrots, scrubbed
50 g/2 oz peas, fresh or frozen
50 g/2 oz fine French beans,
trimmed
1 tbsp olive oil
1 onion, peeled and finely chopped
1 garlic clove, peeled and
finely chopped
2 tsp freshly chopped thyme
225 g/8 oz risotto rice
150 ml/¹/₄ pint white wine
1 tbsp each freshly chopped basil,
chives and parsley
zest of ¹/₂ lemon
3 tbsp crème fraîche
salt and freshly ground
black pepper

Bring the vegetable stock to the boil in a large saucepan and add the asparagus, baby carrots, peas and beans. Bring the stock back to the boil and remove the vegetables at once using a slotted spoon. Rinse under cold running water. Drain again and reserve. Keep the stock hot.

Heat the oil in a large, deep frying pan and add the onion. Cook over a medium heat for 4–5 minutes until starting to brown. Add the garlic and thyme and cook for a further few seconds. Add the rice and stir well for a minute until the rice is hot and coated in oil.

Add the white wine and stir continuously until the wine is almost completely absorbed by the rice. Begin adding the stock a ladleful at a time, stirring well and waiting until the last ladleful has been absorbed before stirring in the next. Add the vegetables after using about half of the stock. Continue until all the stock is used. This will take 20–25 minutes. The rice and vegetables should both be tender.

Remove the pan from the heat. Stir in the herbs, lemon zest and crème fraîche. Season to taste with salt and pepper and serve immediately.

Rice Nuggets in Herby Tomato Sauce

Serves 4

600 ml/1 pint vegetable stock
1 bay leaf
175 g/6 oz arborio rice
50 g/2 oz vegetarian cheddar
cheese, grated
1 medium egg yolk
1 tbsp plain flour
2 tbsp freshly chopped parsley
salt and freshly ground
black pepper
grated vegetarian Italian hard
cheese, to serve

For the herby tomato sauce:

1 tbsp olive oil
1 onion, peeled and thinly sliced
1 garlic clove, peeled and crushed
1 small yellow pepper, deseeded
and diced
400 g can chopped tomatoes
1 tbsp freshly chopped basil

Pour the stock into a large saucepan. Add the bay leaf. Bring to the boil, add the rice, stir, then cover and simmer for 15 minutes.

Uncover, reduce the heat to low and cook for a further 5 minutes until the rice is tender and all the stock is absorbed, stirring frequently towards the end of cooking time. Cool.

Stir the cheese, egg yolk, flour and parsley into the rice. Season to taste, then shape into 20 walnut-size balls. Cover and refrigerate.

To make the sauce, heat the oil in a large frying pan and cook the onion for 5 minutes. Add the garlic and yellow pepper and cook for a further 5 minutes until soft.

Stir in the chopped tomatoes and simmer gently for 3 minutes. Stir in the chopped basil and season to taste.

Add the rice nuggets to the sauce and simmer for a further 10 minutes, or until the rice nuggets are cooked through and the sauce has reduced a little. Spoon onto serving plates and serve hot, sprinkled with grated vegetarian Italian hard cheese.

Aduki Bean & Rice Burgers

Serves 4

2¹/₂ tbsp sunflower oil
1 medium onion, peeled and very
finely chopped
1 garlic clove, peeled and crushed
1 tsp curry paste
225 g/8 oz basmati rice
400 g can aduki beans, drained
and rinsed
225 ml/8 fl oz vegetable stock
125 g/4 oz firm tofu, crumbled
1 tsp garam masala
2 tbsp freshly chopped coriander
salt and freshly ground
black pepper

For the carrot raita:

2 large carrots, peeled and grated
¹/₂ cucumber, cut into tiny dice
150 ml/¹/₄ pint Greek yogurt

To serve:

wholemeal baps
tomato slices
lettuce leaves

Heat 1 tablespoon of the oil in a saucepan and gently cook the onion for 10 minutes until soft. Add the garlic and curry paste and cook for a few more seconds. Stir in the rice and beans.

Pour in the stock, bring to the boil and simmer for 12 minutes, or until all the stock has been absorbed – do not lift the lid for the first 10 minutes of cooking. Reserve.

Lightly mash the tofu. Add to the rice mixture with the garam masala, coriander, salt and pepper. Mix.

Divide the mixture into 8 and shape into burgers. Chill in the refrigerator for 30 minutes.

Meanwhile, make the raita. Mix together the carrots, cucumber and Greek yogurt. Spoon into a small bowl and chill in the refrigerator until ready to serve.

Heat the remaining oil in a large frying pan. Fry the burgers, in batches if necessary, for 4–5 minutes on each side until lightly browned. Serve in the baps with tomato slices and lettuce. Accompany with the raita.

Wild Rice Dolmades

Serves 4–6

6 tbsp olive oil
25 g/1 oz pine nuts
175 g/6 oz mushrooms, wiped and
finely chopped
4 spring onions, trimmed and
finely chopped
1 garlic clove, peeled and crushed
50 g/2 oz cooked wild rice
2 tsp freshly chopped dill
2 tsp freshly chopped mint
salt and freshly ground
black pepper
16–24 prepared medium vine leaves
about 300 ml/¹/₂ pint vegetable stock

To garnish:

lemon wedges
fresh dill sprigs

Heat 1 tablespoon of the oil in a frying pan and gently cook the pine nuts for 2–3 minutes, stirring frequently, until golden. Remove from the pan and reserve.

Add 1¹/₂ tablespoons of the oil to the pan and gently cook the mushrooms, spring onions and garlic for 7–8 minutes until very soft. Stir in the rice, herbs, salt and pepper.

Put a heaped teaspoon of stuffing in the centre of each leaf (if the leaves are small, put two together, overlapping slightly). Fold over the stalk end, then the sides and roll up to make a neat parcel. Continue until all the stuffing is used.

Arrange the stuffed vine leaves close together seam-side down in a large saucepan, drizzling each with a little of the remaining oil – there will be several layers. Pour over just enough stock to cover. Put an inverted plate over the dolmades to stop them unrolling during cooking. Bring to the boil, then simmer very gently for 3 minutes. Cool in the saucepan.

Transfer the dolmades to a serving dish. Cover and chill in the refrigerator before serving. Sprinkle with the pine nuts and garnish with lemon and dill. Serve.

Rice-filled Peppers

Serves 4

8 ripe tomatoes
2 tbsp olive oil
1 onion, peeled and chopped
1 garlic clove, peeled and crushed
$\frac{1}{2}$ tsp dark muscovado sugar
125 g/4 oz cooked long-grain rice
50 g/2 oz pine nuts, toasted
1 tbsp freshly chopped oregano
salt and freshly ground black pepper
2 large red peppers
2 large yellow peppers

To serve:

mixed salad
crusty bread

Preheat the oven to 200°C/400°F/Gas Mark 6. Cut crosses onto the tops of the tomatoes, then place them in a small bowl and pour over boiling water to cover. Leave for 1 minute, then drain. Plunge the tomatoes into cold water to cool, then peel off the skins. Quarter, remove the seeds and chop.

Heat the olive oil in a frying pan and cook the onion gently for 10 minutes until softened. Add the garlic, chopped tomatoes and sugar. Gently cook the tomato mixture for 10 minutes until thickened. Remove from the heat and stir the rice, pine nuts and oregano into the sauce. Season to taste with salt and pepper.

Halve the peppers lengthways, cutting through and leaving the stem on. Remove the seeds and cores, then put the peppers in a lightly oiled roasting tin, cut-side down, and cook in the preheated oven for about 10 minutes.

Turn the peppers so they are cut-side up. Spoon in the filling, then cover with kitchen foil. Return to the oven for 15 minutes, or until the peppers are very tender, removing the foil for the last 5 minutes to allow the tops to brown a little.

Serve one red pepper half and one yellow pepper half per person with a mixed salad and plenty of warm, crusty bread.

Chinese Egg Fried Rice

Serves 4

250 g/9 oz long-grain rice
1 tbsp dark sesame oil
2 large eggs
1 tbsp sunflower oil
2 garlic cloves, peeled and crushed
2.5 cm/1 inch piece fresh root ginger, peeled and grated
1 carrot, peeled and cut into matchsticks
125 g/4 oz mangetout, halved
220 g can water chestnuts, drained and halved
1 yellow pepper, deseeded and diced
4 spring onions, trimmed and finely shredded
2 tbsp light soy sauce
1/2 tsp paprika
salt and freshly ground black pepper

Bring a saucepan of lightly salted water to the boil, add the rice and cook for 15 minutes, or according to the packet instructions. Drain and leave to cool.

Heat a wok or large frying pan and add the sesame oil. Beat the eggs in a small bowl and pour into the hot wok. Using a fork, draw the egg in from the sides of the pan to the centre until it sets, then turn over and cook the other side. When set and golden, turn out onto a board. Leave to cool, then cut into very thin strips.

Wipe the wok clean with absorbent kitchen paper, return to the heat and add the sunflower oil. When hot, add the garlic and ginger and stir-fry for 30 seconds. Add the remaining vegetables and continue to stir-fry for 3–4 minutes until tender but still crisp.

Stir the reserved cooked rice into the wok with the soy sauce and paprika and season to taste with salt and pepper. Fold in the cooked egg strips and heat through. Tip into a warm serving dish and serve immediately.

Beetroot Risotto

Serves 6

6 tbsp extra virgin olive oil
1 onion, peeled and finely chopped
2 garlic cloves, peeled and
finely chopped
2 tsp freshly chopped thyme
1 tsp grated lemon zest
350 g/12 oz arborio rice
150 ml/$\frac{1}{4}$ pint dry white wine
900 ml/1$\frac{1}{2}$ pints vegetable
stock, heated
2 tbsp double cream
225 g/8 oz cooked beetroot, peeled
and finely chopped
2 tbsp freshly chopped parsley
75 g/3 oz vegetarian Italian hard
cheese, freshly grated
salt and freshly ground
black pepper
fresh thyme sprigs, to garnish

Heat half the oil in a large, heavy-based frying pan. Add the onion, garlic, thyme and lemon zest. Cook for 5 minutes, stirring frequently, until the onion is soft and transparent but not coloured. Add the rice and stir until it is well coated in the oil.

Add the wine, then bring to the boil and boil rapidly until the wine has almost completely evaporated. Reduce the heat.

Keeping the pan over a low heat, add a ladleful of the hot stock to the rice and cook, stirring continuously, until the stock is absorbed. Continue gradually adding the stock in this way until the rice is tender; this should take about 20 minutes. You may not need all the stock.

Stir in the cream, chopped beetroot, parsley and half the grated Italian hard cheese. Season to taste with salt and pepper. Garnish with sprigs of fresh thyme and serve immediately with the remaining grated cheese.

Basmati Rice with Saffron & Broad Beans

Serves 4

1 medium egg
2 tbsp olive oil
1 tbsp freshly chopped mixed herbs
salt and freshly ground
black pepper
200 g/7 oz basmati rice
50 g/2 oz butter
1 small onion, peeled and
finely chopped
1 garlic clove, peeled and
finely chopped
large pinch saffron strands
225 g/8 oz shelled broad beans,
blanched

Beat the egg with 1 teaspoon of the olive oil and the herbs. Season lightly with salt and pepper. Heat the remaining teaspoon of olive oil in a wok or small frying pan. Pour half the egg mixture into the pan, tilting it to coat the bottom. Cook gently until set on top. Flip over and cook for a further 30 seconds. Transfer to a plate and repeat, using the remaining mixture, then reserve.

Wash the rice in several changes of water until the water remains relatively clear. Add the drained rice to a large saucepan of boiling salted water and cook for 12–15 minutes until tender. Drain well and reserve.

Heat the butter with the remaining oil in a wok and add the onion and garlic. Cook gently for 3–4 minutes until the onion is softened. Add the saffron and stir well. Add the drained rice and stir before adding the broad beans. Cook for a further 2–3 minutes until heated through.

Meanwhile, roll the egg pancakes into cigar shapes, then slice crossways into strips. To serve, divide the rice between individual serving bowls and top with the egg strips.

Red Lentil Kedgeree
with Avocado & Tomatoes

Serves 4

150 g/5 oz basmati rice
150 g/5 oz red lentils
15 g/½ oz butter
1 tbsp sunflower oil
1 medium onion, peeled and
chopped
1 tsp ground cumin
4 cardamom pods, bruised
1 bay leaf
450 ml/³/₄ pint vegetable stock
1 ripe avocado, peeled, stoned
and diced
1 tbsp lemon juice
4 plum tomatoes, peeled and diced
2 tbsp freshly chopped coriander
salt and freshly ground black pepper
lemon or lime slices, to garnish

Put the rice and lentils in a sieve and rinse under cold running water. Tip into a bowl, then pour over enough cold water to cover and leave to soak for 10 minutes.

Heat the butter and oil in a saucepan. Add the sliced onion and cook gently, stirring occasionally, for 10 minutes until softened. Stir in the cumin, cardamom pods and bay leaf and cook for a further minute, stirring all the time.

Drain the rice and lentils, rinse again and add to the onions in the saucepan. Stir in the vegetable stock and bring to the boil. Reduce the heat, cover the saucepan and simmer for 14–15 minutes until the rice and lentils are tender.

Place the diced avocado in a bowl and toss with the lemon juice. Stir in the tomatoes and chopped coriander. Season to taste with salt and pepper.

Fluff up the rice with a fork, spoon into a warm serving dish and spoon the avocado mixture on top. Garnish with lemon or lime slices and serve.

Brown Rice Spiced Pilaf

Serves 4

1 tbsp vegetable oil
1 tbsp blanched almonds, flaked
or chopped
1 onion, peeled and chopped
1 carrot, peeled and diced
225 g/8 oz flat mushrooms,
thickly sliced
$\frac{1}{4}$ tsp ground cinnamon
large pinch dried chilli flakes
50 g/2 oz dried apricots, roughly
chopped
25 g/1 oz currants
zest of 1 orange
350 g/12 oz brown basmati rice
900 ml/1$\frac{1}{2}$ pints vegetable stock
2 tbsp freshly chopped coriander
2 tbsp freshly snipped chives
salt and freshly ground black pepper
snipped chives, to garnish

Preheat the oven to 200°C/400°F/Gas Mark 6. Heat the oil in a large, flameproof casserole dish and add the almonds. Cook for 1–2 minutes until just browning. (Be very careful, as the nuts will burn very easily).

Add the onion and carrot. Cook for 5 minutes until softened and starting to turn brown. Add the mushrooms and cook for a further 5 minutes, stirring often.

Add the cinnamon and chilli flakes and cook for about 30 seconds before adding the apricots, currants, orange zest and rice.

Stir together well and add the stock. Bring to the boil, cover tightly and transfer to the preheated oven. Cook for 45 minutes until the rice and vegetables are tender.

Stir the coriander and chives into the pilaf and season to taste with salt and pepper. Garnish with the extra chives and serve immediately.

Calypso Rice with Curried Bananas

Serves 4

2 tbsp sunflower oil
1 medium onion, peeled and
finely chopped
1 garlic clove, peeled and crushed
1 red chilli, deseeded
and finely chopped
1 red pepper, deseeded
and chopped
225 g/8 oz basmati rice
juice of 1 lime
350 ml/12 fl oz vegetable stock
200 g can black-eye beans, drained
and rinsed
2 tbsp freshly chopped parsley
salt and freshly ground black pepper
coriander sprigs, to garnish

For the curried bananas:

4 green bananas
2 tbsp sunflower oil
200 ml/7 fl oz coconut milk
2 tsp mild curry paste

Heat the oil in a large frying pan and gently cook the onion for 10 minutes until soft. Add the garlic, chilli and red pepper and cook for 2–3 minutes.

Rinse the rice under cold running water, then add to the pan and stir. Pour in the lime juice and stock, bring to the boil, cover and simmer for 12–15 minutes until the rice is tender and the stock is absorbed. Stir in the beans and parsley and season to taste with salt and pepper. Leave to stand, covered, for 5 minutes before serving, to allow the beans to warm through.

While the rice is cooking, make the curried green bananas. Remove the skins from the bananas – they may need to be cut off with a sharp knife. Slice the flesh thickly. Heat the oil in a frying pan and cook the bananas in two batches for 2–3 minutes, until lightly browned, then reserve. Pour the coconut milk into the pan and stir in the curry paste. Add the banana slices to the coconut milk and simmer, uncovered, over a low heat for 8–10 minutes until the bananas are very soft and the coconut milk slightly reduced.

Spoon the rice onto warm serving plates, garnish with coriander and serve immediately with the curried bananas.

Mixed Grain Pilaf

Serves 4

2 tbsp olive oil
1 garlic clove, peeled and crushed
$\frac{1}{2}$ tsp ground turmeric
125 g/4 oz mixed long-grain
and wild rice
50 g/2 oz red lentils
300 ml/½ pint vegetable stock
200 g can chopped tomatoes
5 cm/2 inch piece
cinnamon stick
salt and freshly ground
black pepper
400 g can mixed beans, drained
and rinsed
15 g/¹/₂ oz butter
1 bunch spring onions, trimmed and
finely sliced
3 medium eggs
4 tbsp freshly chopped herbs,
such as parsley and chervil
fresh dill sprigs,
to garnish

Heat 1 tablespoon of the oil in a saucepan. Add the garlic and turmeric and cook for a few seconds. Stir in the rice and lentils. Add the stock, tomatoes and cinnamon. Season to taste with salt and pepper. Stir once and bring to the boil. Lower the heat, cover and simmer for 20 minutes until most of the stock is absorbed and the rice and lentils are tender. Stir in the beans, replace the lid and leave to stand for 2–3 minutes to allow the beans to heat through.

While the rice is cooking, heat the remaining oil and butter in a frying pan. Add the spring onions and cook for 4–5 minutes until soft. Lightly beat the eggs with 2 tablespoons of the herbs, then season with salt and pepper.

Pour the egg mixture over the spring onions. Stir gently with a spatula over a low heat, drawing the mixture from the sides to the centre as the omelette sets. When almost set, stop stirring and cook for about 30 seconds until golden underneath.

Remove the omelette from the pan, roll up and slice into thin strips. Fluff the rice up with a fork and remove the cinnamon stick. Spoon onto serving plates, top with strips of omelette and the remaining chopped herbs. Garnish with sprigs of dill and serve.

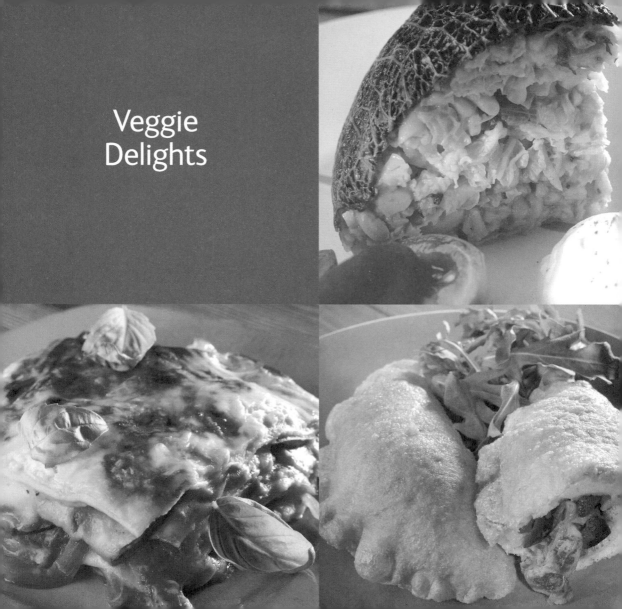

Veggie
Delights

If you're the sort of vegetarian who can't get enough veggies, then this is the section for you. These recipes are heavily laden with almost every vegetable under the sun – try the Aubergine & Tomato Layer, or the Light Ratatouille when you're in need of a little bit of comfort food!

Gnocchi Roulade with Mozzarella & Spinach

Serves 8

600 ml/1 pint milk
125 g/4 oz fine semolina or polenta
25 g/1 oz butter
75 g/3 oz vegetarian cheddar cheese, grated
2 medium egg yolks
salt and freshly ground black pepper
700 g/1¹/₂ lb baby spinach leaves
¹/₂ tsp freshly grated nutmeg
150 g/5 oz vegetarian mozzarella cheese, grated
2 tbsp freshly grated vegetarian Italian hard cheese
freshly made tomato sauce, to serve (*see* page 220)

Preheat the oven to 240°C/475°F/Gas Mark 9, 15 minutes before cooking. Oil and line a large Swiss roll tin (23 cm x 33 cm/9 inches x 13 inches) with nonstick baking parchment.

Pour the milk into a heavy-based pan and whisk in the semolina. Bring to the boil, then simmer, stirring continuously with a wooden spoon, for 3–4 minutes until very thick. Remove from the heat and stir in the butter and cheddar cheese until melted. Whisk in the egg yolks and season to taste with salt and pepper. Pour into the lined tin. Cover and allow to cool for 1 hour.

Cook the baby spinach in batches in a large pan with 1 teaspoon water for 3–4 minutes, or until wilted. Drain thoroughly, season to taste with salt, pepper and nutmeg, then allow to cool.

Spread the spinach over the cooled semolina mixture and sprinkle over 75 g/3 oz of the mozzarella and half the Italian hard cheese. Bake in the preheated oven for 20 minutes, or until golden.

Allow to cool, then roll up like a Swiss roll. Sprinkle with the remaining mozzarella and Italian hard cheese, then bake for another 15–20 minutes until golden. Serve immediately with freshly made tomato sauce.

Cabbage Timbale

Serves 4–6

1 small savoy cabbage, weighing
about 350 g/12 oz
2 tbsp olive oil
1 leek, trimmed and chopped
1 garlic clove, peeled and crushed
75 g/3 oz long-grain rice
200 g can chopped tomatoes
300 ml/¹/₂ pint vegetable stock
400 g can flageolet beans, drained
and rinsed
75 g/3 oz vegetarian cheddar
cheese, grated
1 tbsp freshly chopped oregano
salt and freshly ground
black pepper

To garnish:

Greek yogurt with paprika
tomato wedges

Preheat the oven to 180°C/350°F/Gas Mark 4, 10 minutes before required. Remove six of the outer leaves of the cabbage. Cut off the thickest part of the stalk and blanch the leaves in lightly salted boiling water for 2 minutes. Lift out with a slotted spoon and briefly rinse under cold water and reserve. Remove the stalks from the rest of the cabbage leaves. Shred the leaves and blanch in the boiling water for 1 minute. Drain, rinse under cold water and pat dry on absorbent kitchen paper.

Heat the oil in a frying pan and cook the leek and garlic for 5 minutes. Stir in the rice, chopped tomatoes with their juice and the stock. Bring to the boil, cover and simmer for 15 minutes. Remove the lid and simmer for a further 4–5 minutes, stirring frequently, until the liquid is absorbed and the rice is tender. Stir in the flageolet beans, cheese and oregano. Season to taste with salt and pepper.

Line an oiled 1.1 litre/2 pint pudding basin with some of the large cabbage leaves, overlapping them slightly. Fill the basin with alternate layers of rice mixture and shredded leaves, pressing down well. Cover the top with the remaining leaves. Cover with oiled kitchen foil and bake in the preheated oven for 30 minutes. Leave to stand for 10 minutes. Turn out, cut into wedges and serve with yogurt sprinkled with paprika and tomato wedges.

Light Ratatouille

Serves 4

1 red pepper
2 courgettes, trimmed
1 small aubergine, trimmed
1 onion, peeled
2 ripe tomatoes
50 g/2 oz button mushrooms, wiped
and halved or quartered
200 ml/7 fl oz tomato juice
1 tbsp freshly chopped basil
salt and freshly ground
black pepper

Deseed the pepper, remove the membrane with a small, sharp knife and cut into small dice. Thickly slice the courgettes and cut the aubergine into small dice. Slice the onion into rings.

Cut a cross in the tops of the tomatoes and place them in boiling water until their skins begin to peel away. Remove the skins from the tomatoes, cut into quarters and remove the seeds.

Place all the vegetables in a saucepan with the tomato juice and basil. Season to taste with salt and pepper. Bring to the boil, cover and simmer for 15 minutes, or until the vegetables are tender.

Remove the vegetables with a slotted spoon and arrange in a large serving dish.

Bring the liquid in the pan to the boil and boil for 20 seconds until it is slightly thickened. Season the sauce to taste with salt and pepper.

Pass the sauce through a sieve to remove some of the seeds and pour over the vegetables. Serve the ratatouille hot or cold.

Marinated Vegetable Kebabs

Serves 4

2 small courgettes, cut into
2 cm/³/₄ inch pieces
¹/₂ green pepper, deseeded and cut
into 2.5 cm/1 inch pieces
¹/₂ red pepper, deseeded and cut
into 2.5 cm/1 inch pieces
¹/₂ yellow pepper, deseeded and cut
into 2.5 cm/1 inch pieces
8 baby onions, peeled
8 button mushrooms
8 cherry tomatoes
freshly chopped parsley, to garnish
freshly cooked couscous, to serve

For the marinade:

1 tbsp light olive oil
4 tbsp dry sherry
2 tbsp light soy sauce
1 red chilli, deseeded and
finely chopped
2 garlic cloves, peeled and crushed
2.5 cm/1 inch piece root ginger,
peeled and finely grated

Place the courgettes, peppers and baby onions in a pan of just boiled water. Bring back to the boil and simmer for about 30 seconds. Drain and rinse the cooked vegetables in cold water and dry on absorbent kitchen paper.

Thread the cooked vegetables and the mushrooms and tomatoes alternately onto skewers and place in a large, shallow dish.

Make the marinade by whisking all the ingredients together until thoroughly blended. Pour the marinade evenly over the kebabs, then chill in the refrigerator for at least 1 hour. Spoon the marinade over the kebabs occasionally during this time.

Place the kebabs in a hot griddle pan or on a hot barbecue and cook gently for 10–12 minutes. Turn the kebabs frequently and brush with the marinade when needed. When the vegetables are tender, sprinkle over the chopped parsley and serve immediately with couscous.

Vegetarian Cassoulet

Serves 6

225 g/8 oz dried haricot beans,
soaked overnight
2 medium onions, peeled and
one chopped
1 bay leaf
1.5 litres/2¹/₂ pints cold water
575 g/1¹/₄ lb large potatoes, peeled
and cut into 1 cm/ ¹/₂ inch slices
5 tsp olive oil
1 large garlic clove, peeled
and crushed
2 leeks, trimmed and sliced
200 g can chopped tomatoes
1 tsp dark muscovado sugar
1 tbsp freshly chopped thyme
2 tbsp freshly chopped parsley
salt and freshly ground black pepper
3 courgettes, trimmed and sliced

For the topping:

50 g/2 oz fresh white breadcrumbs
25 g/1 oz vegetarian cheddar
cheese, finely grated

Preheat the oven to 180°C/350°F/Gas Mark 4, 10 minutes before required. Drain the beans, rinse under cold running water and put in a saucepan. Add the whole onion to the beans with the bay leaf. Pour in the water. Bring to a rapid boil and cook for 10 minutes, then turn down the heat, cover and simmer for 50 minutes, or until the beans are almost tender. Drain the beans, reserving the liquor, but discarding the onion and bay leaf.

Cook the potatoes in a saucepan of lightly salted boiling water for 6–7 minutes until almost tender when tested with the point of a knife. Drain and reserve.

Heat the oil in a frying pan and cook the chopped onion with the garlic and leeks for 10 minutes until softened. Stir in the tomatoes, sugar, thyme and parsley. Stir in the beans with 300 ml/¹/₂ pint of the reserved liquor and season to taste. Simmer, uncovered, for 5 minutes.

Layer the potato slices, courgettes and ladlefuls of the bean mixture in a large, flameproof casserole dish. To make the topping, mix together the breadcrumbs and cheese and sprinkle over the top. Bake in the preheated oven for 40 minutes, or until the vegetables are cooked through and the topping is golden brown and crisp. Serve immediately.

Melanzane Parmigiana

Serves 4

900 g/2 lb aubergines
salt and freshly ground black pepper
5 tbsp olive oil
1 red onion, peeled and chopped
$^1/_2$ tsp mild paprika pepper
150 ml/$^1/_4$ pint dry red wine
150 ml/$^1/_4$ pint vegetable stock
400 g can chopped tomatoes
1 tsp tomato purée
1 tbsp freshly chopped oregano
175 g/6 oz vegetarian mozzarella
cheese, thinly sliced
40 g/1$^1/_2$ oz vegetarian Italian hard
cheese, grated
fresh basil sprig, to garnish

Preheat the oven to 200°C/400°F/Gas Mark 6, 15 minutes before cooking. Cut the aubergines lengthways into thin slices. Sprinkle with salt and leave to drain in a colander over a bowl for 30 minutes.

Meanwhile, heat 1 tablespoon of the olive oil in a saucepan and fry the onion for 10 minutes until softened. Add the paprika and cook for 1 minute. Stir in the wine, stock, tomatoes and tomato purée. Simmer, uncovered, for 25 minutes, or until fairly thick. Stir in the oregano and season to taste with salt and pepper. Remove from the heat.

Rinse the aubergine slices thoroughly under cold water and pat dry on absorbent kitchen paper. Heat 2 tablespoons of the oil in a griddle pan and cook the aubergines in batches, for 3 minutes on each side, until golden. Drain well on absorbent kitchen paper.

Pour half of the tomato sauce into the base of a large, ovenproof dish. Cover with half the aubergine slices, then top with the mozzarella. Cover with the remaining aubergine slices and pour over the remaining tomato sauce. Sprinkle with the grated Italian hard cheese. Bake in the preheated oven for 30 minutes, or until the aubergines are tender and the sauce is bubbling. Garnish with a sprig of fresh basil and cool for a few minutes before serving.

Spinach Dumplings with Rich Tomato Sauce

Serves 4

For the sauce:

2 tbsp olive oil
1 onion, peeled and chopped
1 garlic clove, peeled and crushed
1 red chilli, deseeded and chopped
150 ml/¹/₄ pint dry white wine
400 g can chopped tomatoes
pared strip lemon zest

For the dumplings:

450 g/1 lb fresh spinach
50 g/2 oz ricotta cheese
25 g/1 oz fresh white breadcrumbs
25 g/1 oz vegetarian Italian hard
cheese, grated
1 medium egg yolk
¹/₄ tsp freshly grated nutmeg
salt and freshly ground black pepper
5 tbsp plain flour
2 tbsp olive oil, for frying
fresh basil leaves, to garnish
freshly cooked tagliatelle, to serve

To make the tomato sauce, heat the olive oil in a large saucepan and fry the onion gently for 5 minutes. Add the garlic and chilli and cook for a further 5 minutes until softened.

Stir in the wine, chopped tomatoes and lemon zest. Bring to the boil, cover and simmer for 20 minutes, then uncover and simmer for 15 minutes, or until the sauce has thickened. Remove the lemon rind and season to taste with salt and pepper.

To make the spinach dumplings, wash the spinach thoroughly and remove any tough stalks. Cover and cook in a large saucepan over a low heat with just the water clinging to the leaves. Drain, then squeeze out all the excess water. Finely chop and put in a large bowl.

Add the ricotta, breadcrumbs, Italian hard cheese and egg yolk to the spinach. Season with nutmeg, salt and pepper. Mix together and shape into 20 walnut-size balls.

Toss the spinach balls in the flour. Heat the olive oil in a large, nonstick frying pan and fry the balls gently for 5–6 minutes, carefully turning occasionally. Garnish with fresh basil leaves and serve immediately with the tomato sauce and tagliatelle.

Aubergine Cannelloni with Watercress Sauce

Serves 4

4 large aubergines, about
250 g/9 oz each
5–6 tbsp olive oil
350 g/12 oz vegetarian ricotta cheese
75 g/3 oz vegetarian Italian hard
cheese, grated
3 tbsp freshly chopped basil
salt and freshly ground
black pepper

For the watercress sauce:

75 g/3 oz watercress, trimmed
200 ml/⅓ pint vegetable stock
1 shallot, peeled and sliced
pared strip lemon zest
1 large thyme sprig
3 tbsp crème fraîche
1 tsp lemon juice

To garnish:

watercress sprigs
lemon zest

Preheat the oven to 190°C/375°F/Gas Mark 5, 10 minutes before cooking. Cut the aubergines lengthways into thin slices, discarding the side pieces. Heat 2 tablespoons of the oil in a frying pan and cook the slices in a single layer in batches, turning once, until golden on both sides.

Mix the cheeses, basil and seasoning together. Lay the aubergine slices on a clean surface and spread the cheese mixture evenly between them. Roll up the slices from one of the short ends to enclose the filling. Place seam-side down in a single layer in an ovenproof dish. Bake in the preheated oven for 15 minutes, or until golden.

To make the watercress sauce, blanch the watercress leaves in boiling water for about 30 seconds. Drain well, then rinse in a sieve under cold running water and squeeze dry. Put the stock, shallot, lemon zest and thyme in a small saucepan. Boil rapidly until reduced by half, then remove from the heat and strain. Put the watercress and strained stock in a food processor and blend until fairly smooth. Return to the saucepan, stir in the crème fraîche and lemon juice and season to taste with salt and pepper. Heat gently until the sauce is piping hot. Serve a little of the sauce drizzled over the aubergines and the rest separately in a jug. Garnish the cannelloni with sprigs of watercress and lemon zest. Serve immediately.

Vegetable Frittata

Serves 2

6 medium eggs
2 tbsp freshly chopped parsley
1 tbsp freshly chopped tarragon
25 g/1 oz pecorino or vegetarian
Italian hard cheese, finely grated
freshly ground black pepper
175 g/6 oz tiny new potatoes
2 small carrots, peeled and sliced
125 g/4 oz broccoli, cut
into small florets
1 courgette, about 125 g/4 oz, sliced
2 tbsp olive oil
4 spring onions, trimmed and
thinly sliced

To serve:

mixed green salad
crusty Italian bread

Preheat the grill just before cooking. Lightly beat the eggs with the parsley, tarragon and half the cheese. Season to taste with black pepper and reserve. (Salt is not needed, as the pecorino is very salty.)

Bring a large saucepan of lightly salted water to the boil. Add the new potatoes and cook for 8 minutes. Add the carrots and cook for 4 minutes, then add the broccoli florets and the courgette and cook for a further 3–4 minutes until all the vegetables are barely tender. Drain well.

Heat the oil in a 20.5 cm/8 inch heavy-based frying pan. Add the spring onions and cook for 3–4 minutes until softened. Add all the vegetables and cook for a few seconds, then pour in the beaten egg mixture. Stir gently for about a minute, then cook for a further 1–2 minutes until the bottom of the frittata is set and golden brown.

Place the pan under a hot grill for 1 minute, or until almost set and just beginning to brown. Sprinkle with the remaining cheese and grill for a further 1 minute, or until it is lightly browned. Loosen the edges and slide out of the pan. Cut into wedges and serve hot or warm with a mixed green salad and crusty Italian bread.

Panzerotti

Serves 16

450 g/1 lb strong white flour
pinch salt
1 tsp easy-blend dried yeast
2 tbsp olive oil
300 ml/¹/₂ pint warm water
fresh rocket leaves, to serve

For the filling:

1 tbsp olive oil
1 small red onion, peeled and
finely chopped
2 garlic cloves, peeled and crushed
¹/₂ yellow pepper, deseeded
and chopped
1 small courgette, about 75 g/3 oz,
trimmed and chopped
50 g/2 oz black olives, pitted
and quartered
125 g/4 oz vegetarian mozzarella
cheese, cut into tiny cubes
salt and freshly ground black pepper
5–6 tbsp tomato purée
1 tsp dried mixed herbs
oil, for deep-frying

Sift the flour and salt into a bowl. Stir in the yeast. Make a well in the centre. Add the oil and the warm water and mix to a soft dough. Knead on a lightly floured surface until smooth and elastic. Put in an oiled bowl, cover and leave in a warm place to rise while making the filling. To make the filling, heat the oil in a frying pan and cook the onion for 5 minutes. Add the garlic, yellow pepper and courgette. Cook for about 5 minutes until the vegetables are tender. Tip into a bowl and leave to cool slightly. Stir in the olives and mozzarella cheese and season to taste with salt and pepper.

Briefly reknead the dough. Divide into 16 equal pieces. Roll out each to a circle about 10 cm/4 inches. Mix together the tomato purée and dried herbs, then spread about 1 teaspoon on each circle, leaving a 2 cm/³/₄ inch border around the edge. Divide the filling equally between the circles; it will seem a small amount, but if you overfill, they will leak during cooking. Brush the edges with water, then fold in half to enclose the filling. Press to seal, then crimp the edges. Heat the oil in a deep-fat fryer to 180°C/350°F. Deep-fry the panzerotti in batches for 3 minutes, or until golden. Drain on absorbent kitchen paper and keep warm in a low oven until ready to serve with fresh rocket.

Aubergine & Tomato Layer

Serves 4

2 aubergines, about 700 g/
1¹/₂ lb, trimmed and thinly sliced
6 tbsp olive oil
1 onion, peeled and finely sliced
1 garlic clove, peeled and crushed
400 g can chopped tomatoes
50 ml/2 fl oz red wine
¹/₂ tsp sugar
salt and freshly ground black pepper
50 g/2 oz butter
40 g/1¹/₂ oz flour
450 ml/³/₄ pint milk
225 g/8 oz fresh egg lasagne
125 g/3 oz vegetarian mozzarella
cheese, grated
2 medium eggs, beaten
200 ml/7 fl oz Greek yogurt
fresh basil leaves, to garnish

Preheat the oven to 190°C/375°F/Gas Mark 5, 10 minutes before cooking. Brush the aubergine slices with 5 tablespoons of the olive oil and place on a baking sheet. Bake in the preheated oven for 20 minutes, or until tender. Remove from the oven and increase the temperature to 200°C/400°F/Gas Mark 6.

Heat the remaining oil in a heavy-based pan. Add the onion and garlic, cook for 2–3 minutes, then add the tomatoes, wine and sugar. Season to taste with salt and pepper, then simmer for 20 minutes.

Melt the butter in another pan. Stir in the flour, cook for 2 minutes, then whisk in the milk. Cook for 2–3 minutes until thickened. Season to taste. Pour a little white sauce into a lightly oiled, 1.7 litre/3 pint baking dish. Cover with a layer of lasagne, spread with tomato sauce, then add some of the aubergine slices. Cover thinly with white sauce and sprinkle with a little cheese. Continue to layer in this way, finishing with a layer of lasagne.

Beat together the eggs and yogurt. Season, then pour over the lasagne. Sprinkle with the remaining cheese and bake in the preheated oven for 25–30 minutes until golden. Garnish with basil leaves and serve.

Courgette & Tarragon Tortilla

Serves 6

700 g/1¹/₂ lb potatoes
3 tbsp olive oil
1 onion, peeled and thinly sliced
salt and freshly ground
black pepper
1 courgette, trimmed and
thinly sliced
6 medium eggs
2 tbsp freshly chopped tarragon
tomato wedges, to serve

Peel the potatoes and thinly slice. Dry the slices in a clean tea towel to get them as dry as possible. Heat the oil in a large, heavy-based pan, add the onion and cook for 3 minutes. Add the potatoes with a little salt and pepper, then stir the potatoes and onion lightly to coat in the oil.

Reduce the heat to the lowest possible setting, cover and cook gently for 5 minutes. Turn the potatoes and onion over and continue to cook for a further 5 minutes. Give the pan a shake every now and again to ensure that the potatoes do not stick to the base or burn. Add the courgette, then cover and cook for a further 10 minutes.

Beat the eggs and tarragon together and season to taste with salt and pepper. Pour the egg mixture over the vegetables and return to the heat. Cook on a low heat for up to 20–25 minutes until there is no liquid egg left on the surface of the tortilla.

Turn the tortilla over by inverting it onto the lid or onto a flat plate. Return the pan to the heat and cook for a final 3–5 minutes until the underside is golden brown. If preferred, place the tortilla under a preheated grill for 4 minutes, or until set and golden brown on top. Cut into small squares and serve hot or cold with tomato wedges.

Curries,
Stir-fries &
Noodles

If you're in the mood for something a little more exotic, these vegetarian dishes from around the world are sure to hit the spot! There are some classic recipes like Thai Noodles & Vegetables with Tofu, but also included are dishes you've likely never tasted before. Why don't you give the Okra Moru Curry a go?

Bean & Cashew Stir-fry

Serves 4

3 tbsp sunflower oil
1 onion, peeled and finely chopped
1 celery stalk, trimmed and chopped
2.5 cm/1 inch piece fresh root ginger,
peeled and grated
2 garlic cloves, peeled and crushed
1 red chilli, deseeded
and finely chopped
175 g/6 oz fine French beans,
trimmed and halved
175 g/6 oz mangetout,
sliced diagonally into 3
75 g/3 oz unsalted cashew nuts
1 tsp brown sugar
125 ml/4 fl oz vegetable stock
2 tbsp dry sherry
1 tbsp light soy sauce
1 tsp red wine vinegar
salt and freshly ground
black pepper
freshly chopped coriander,
to garnish

Heat a wok or large frying pan, add the oil and, when hot, add the onion and celery and stir-fry gently for 3–4 minutes until softened.

Add the ginger, garlic and chilli to the wok and stir-fry for 30 seconds. Stir in the French beans and mangetout together with the cashew nuts and continue to stir-fry for 1–2 minutes until the nuts are golden brown.

Dissolve the sugar in the stock, then blend with the sherry, soy sauce and vinegar. Stir into the bean mixture and bring to the boil. Simmer gently, stirring occasionally, for 3–4 minutes until the beans and mangetout are tender but still crisp and the sauce has thickened slightly. Season to taste with salt and pepper. Transfer to a warm serving bowl or spoon onto individual plates. Sprinkle with freshly chopped coriander and serve immediately.

Vegetable Kofta Curry

Serves 6

350 g/12 oz potatoes, peeled
and diced
225 g/8 oz carrots, peeled and
roughly chopped
225 g/8 oz parsnips, peeled and
roughly chopped
1 medium egg, lightly beaten
75 g/3 oz plain flour, sifted
8 tbsp sunflower oil
2 onions, peeled and sliced
2 garlic cloves, peeled and crushed
2.5 cm/1 inch piece fresh root ginger,
peeled and grated
2 tbsp garam masala
2 tbsp tomato paste
300 ml/¹/₂ pint vegetable stock
250 ml/9 fl oz Greekstyle yogurt
3 tbsp freshly chopped coriander
salt and freshly ground black pepper

Bring a saucepan of lightly salted water to the boil. Add the potatoes, carrots and parsnips. Cover and simmer for 12–15 minutes until the vegetables are tender. Drain the vegetables and mash until very smooth. Stir the egg into the vegetable purée, then add the flour and mix to make a stiff paste and reserve.

Heat 2 tablespoons of the oil in a wok and gently cook the onions for 10 minutes. Add the garlic and ginger and cook for a further 2–3 minutes until very soft and just beginning to colour. Sprinkle the garam masala over the onions and stir in. Add the tomato paste and stock. Bring to the boil, cover and simmer gently for 15 minutes.

Meanwhile, heat the remaining oil in a wok or frying pan. Drop in tablespoons of vegetable batter, 4 or 5 at a time and fry, turning often, for 3–4 minutes until brown and crisp. Remove with a slotted spoon and drain on absorbent kitchen paper. Keep warm in a low oven while cooking the rest.

Stir the yogurt and coriander into the onion sauce. Slowly heat to boiling point and season to taste with salt and pepper. Divide the koftas between warm serving plates and spoon over the sauce. Serve immediately.

Curried Potatoes with Spinach

Serves 4–6

300 g/11 oz potatoes, peeled
1 tsp cumin seeds
2 tbsp vegetable oil
1 onion, peeled and chopped
2 garlic cloves, peeled and crushed
1 red chilli, deseeded and
finely chopped
1 tsp ground coriander
$^{1}/_{2}$ tsp ground turmeric
4 tomatoes
450 g/1 lb fresh leaf spinach,
lightly rinsed and chopped
50 ml/2 fl oz water
salt and freshly ground
black pepper

Cut the potatoes into small cubes and reserve. Dry-fry the cumin seeds in a saucepan for 30 seconds, then add the oil and potatoes and cook for 3–5 minutes, stirring, until the potatoes are beginning to turn golden.

Add the onion, garlic and chilli and continue to cook for 2–3 minutes until the onion is beginning to soften. Sprinkle in the ground coriander and turmeric and cook for a further 2 minutes.

Chop the tomatoes and stir into the pan. Cover and cook, stirring occasionally, for 10 minutes, or until the potatoes are tender. Stir in the spinach, water and seasoning, to taste, and cook for 2 minutes, or until the spinach has wilted, then serve.

Spinach Dhal

Serves 4–6

125 g/4 oz split red lentils
2 onions, peeled and chopped
225 g/8 oz potato, peeled and cut
into small chunks
1 green chilli, deseeded
and chopped
1 tsp ground turmeric
175 g/6 oz fresh spinach
2 tomatoes, chopped
2 tbsp vegetable oil
1 tsp mustard seeds
few curry leaves

Rinse the lentils and place in a saucepan with the onions, potato, chilli, 150 ml/¼ pint water and turmeric. Bring to the boil, then reduce the heat, cover and simmer for 15 minutes, or until the lentils are tender and most of the liquid has been absorbed.

Chop the spinach and add to the pan with the tomatoes and cook for a further 5 minutes, or until the spinach has wilted.

Heat the oil in a frying pan, add the mustard seeds and fry for 1 minute, or until they pop. Add the curry leaves, stir well, then stir into the dhal and serve.

Paneer & Pea Curry

Serves 4–6

225 g/8 oz paneer
vegetable oil, for deep-frying,
plus 2 tbsp for shallow-frying
1¹/₂ tsp cumin seeds
1¹/₂ tsp fennel seeds
3 onions, peeled and chopped
3 garlic cloves, peeled and chopped
1–2 red chillies, deseeded
and chopped
1¹/₂ tsp ground turmeric
1¹/₂ tsp ground fenugreek
1¹/₂ tsp garam masala
4 tomatoes, chopped
300 g/11 oz sugar snap peas
50 ml/2 fl oz water (optional)
4 tbsp double cream
2 tbsp freshly chopped coriander

Cut the paneer into small cubes. Heat the oil in a deep-fryer to a temperature of 180˚C/350°F, then deep-fry the paneer cubes for 3–4 minutes until golden brown. Drain on absorbent kitchen paper and reserve.

Heat the 2 tablespoons of oil in a frying pan, add the seeds and fry for 1–2 minutes until they pop. Add the onions, garlic and chillies and continue to fry for 5 minutes, stirring frequently, until slightly softened. Sprinkle in the turmeric, fenugreek and garam masala and cook for a further 5 minutes.

Stir in the chopped tomatoes and sugar snap peas and continue to cook for 10 minutes, or until the peas are tender. Stir in a little water if the mixture is getting too dry. Add the fried paneer and heat for 2–3 minutes before stirring in the cream. Heat gently for 2–3 minutes, then stir in the chopped coriander. Serve.

Egg & Aubergine Curry

Serves 4–6

4 eggs
2 tbsp vegetable oil
1 tsp cumin seeds
2 onions, peeled and chopped
2–3 garlic cloves, deseeded and finely chopped
2 green chillies, deseeded and finely chopped
5 cm/2 inch piece fresh root ginger, peeled and grated
1 tsp ground turmeric
1 tsp ground coriander
1 tsp garam masala
450 g/1 lb baby aubergines, trimmed
400 g/14 oz can chopped tomatoes
4 tbsp double cream
2 tbsp freshly chopped coriander

Place the eggs in a saucepan and cover with cold water. Bring to the boil and continue to boil for 10 minutes. Drain and plunge into cold water and leave until cold. Drain, shell and reserve.

Heat the oil in a saucepan, add the cumin seeds and fry for 30 seconds, or until they pop. Add the onions, garlic, chillies and ginger and cook for 5 minutes, or until the onion has softened. Add the spices and continue to cook for a further 5 minutes.

Halve the baby aubergines and add to the pan with the chopped tomatoes, then simmer gently, stirring occasionally, for 12–15 minutes until the aubergines are tender. Stir in the cream and cook for a further 3 minutes. Cut the eggs into quarters, add to the pan and stir gently. Heat for 2 minutes before sprinkling with chopped coriander and serving.

Okra Moru Curry

Serves 4–6

2 tbsp vegetable oil
2 red chillies, deseeded
and chopped
1 green chilli, deseeded
and chopped
.5 cm/2 inch piece fresh
root ginger, grated
2–3 garlic cloves, peeled
and crushed
2 onions, peeled and cut
into small wedges
1 tsp ground cumin
1 tsp ground coriander
450 g/1 lb okra, trimmed,
and sliced if large
400 g/14 oz can chopped tomatoes
150 ml/¹/₄ pint natural yogurt

¹/₂–1 tsp turmeric

Heat the oil in a heavy-based saucepan, add the chillies and ginger and cook for 2 minutes, stirring frequently. Using a slotted spoon, remove half of the mixture and reserve.

Add the garlic, onions and ground cumin and coriander and cook for a further 5 minutes, stirring frequently. Add the okra and cook, stirring, until the okra is lightly coated in the spices and oil.

Add the chopped tomatoes with their juice, then bring to the boil, reduce the heat, cover and simmer for 12–15 minutes until the okra is tender.

Meanwhile, blend the reserved chilli mixture with the yogurt and turmeric. Pour into a small saucepan and heat gently for 3 minutes. Pour over the okra and serve.

Creamy Vegetable Korma

Serves 4–6

2 tbsp ghee or vegetable oil
1 large onion, peeled and chopped
2 garlic cloves, peeled and crushed
2.5 cm/1 inch piece root ginger,
peeled and grated
4 cardamom pods
2 tsp ground coriander
1 tsp ground cumin
1 tsp ground turmeric
finely grated zest and juice of
$\frac{1}{2}$ lemon
50 g/2 oz ground almonds
400 ml/14 fl oz vegetable stock
450 g/1 lb potatoes, peeled
and diced
450 g/1 lb mixed vegetables, such
as cauliflower, carrots and turnip,
cut into chunks
150 ml/¼ pint double cream
3 tbsp freshly chopped coriander
salt and freshly ground black pepper
naan bread, to serve

Heat the ghee or oil in a large saucepan. Add the onion and cook for 5 minutes. Stir in the garlic and ginger and cook for a further 5 minutes, or until soft and just beginning to colour.

Stir in the cardamom, ground coriander, cumin and turmeric. Continue cooking over a low heat for 1 minute, stirring.

Stir in the lemon zest and juice and the almonds. Blend in the vegetable stock. Slowly bring to the boil, stirring occasionally.

Add the potatoes and vegetables. Bring back to the boil, then reduce the heat, cover and simmer for 35–40 minutes until the vegetables are just tender. Check after 25 minutes and add a little more stock if needed.

Slowly stir in the cream and chopped coriander. Season to taste with salt and pepper. Cook very gently until heated through, but do not boil. Serve immediately with naan bread.

Vegetables in Coconut Milk with Rice Noodles

Serves 4

75 g/3 oz creamed coconut
1 tsp salt
2 tbsp sunflower oil
2 garlic cloves, peeled and
finely chopped
2 red peppers, deseeded
and cut into thin strips
2.5 cm/1 inch piece fresh root ginger,
peeled and cut into thin strips
125 g/4 oz baby sweetcorn
2 tsp cornflour
2 medium ripe but still firm avocados
1 small Cos lettuce, cut into
thick strips
freshly cooked rice noodles, to serve

Roughly chop the creamed coconut, place in a bowl with the salt, then pour over 600 ml/1 pint boiling water. Stir until the coconut has dissolved completely and reserve.

Heat a wok or large frying pan, add the oil and, when hot, add the chopped garlic, sliced peppers and ginger. Cook for 30 seconds, then cover and cook very gently for 10 minutes, or until the peppers are soft.

Pour in the reserved coconut milk and bring to the boil. Stir in the baby sweetcorn, cover and simmer for 5 minutes. Blend the cornflour with 2 teaspoons water, pour into the wok and cook, stirring, for 2 minutes, or until thickened slightly.

Cut the avocados in half, peel, remove the stones and slice. Add to the wok with the lettuce strips and stir until well mixed and heated through. Serve immediately on a bed of rice noodles.

Thai Noodles & Vegetables with Tofu

Serves 4

225 g/8 oz firm tofu
2 tbsp soy sauce
zest of 1 lime, grated
2 lemongrass stalks
1 red chilli
1 litre/1³/₄ pints vegetable stock
2 slices fresh root ginger, peeled
2 garlic cloves, peeled
2 fresh coriander sprigs
175 g/6 oz dried thread egg noodles
125 g/4 oz shiitake or button
mushrooms, sliced if large
2 carrots, peeled and
cut into matchsticks
125 g/4 oz mangetout
125 g/4 oz pak choi or
other Chinese leaf
1 tbsp freshly chopped coriander
salt and freshly ground black pepper
coriander sprigs, to garnish

Drain the tofu well and cut into cubes. Put into a shallow dish with the soy sauce and lime zest. Stir well to coat and leave to marinate for 30 minutes.

Meanwhile, put the lemongrass and chilli on a chopping board and bruise with the side of a large knife, ensuring the blade is pointing away from you. Put the vegetable stock in a large saucepan and add the lemongrass, chilli, ginger, garlic and coriander. Bring to the boil, cover and simmer gently for 20 minutes.

Strain the stock into a clean pan. Return to the boil and add the noodles, tofu and its marinade and the mushrooms. Simmer gently for 4 minutes.

Add the carrots, mangetout, pak choi and coriander and simmer for a further 3–4 minutes until the vegetables are just tender. Season to taste with salt and pepper. Garnish with coriander sprigs. Serve immediately.

Index

Gnocchi Roulade with Mozzarella & Spinach 208
Layered Cheese & Herb Potato Cake 96
Leek & Potato Tart 170
Mediterranean Potato Salad 50
Potato & Goats' Cheese Tart 158
Roasted Mixed Vegetables with Garlic & Herb Sauce 92
Swede, Turnip, Parsnip & Potato Soup 104
Sweet Potato Cakes with Mango & Tomato Salsa 82
Spinach Dhal 240
Vegetable Frittata 224
Vegetable Kofta Curry 236
Vegetarian Cassoulet 216
Potato & Goats' Cheese Tart 158

R
Red Lentil Kedgeree with Avocado & Tomatoes 198
Red Pepper & Basil Tart 164
rice
    Aduki Bean & Rice Burgers 186
    Basmati Rice with Saffron & Broad Beans 196
    Beetroot Risotto 194
    Brown Rice Spiced Pilaf 200
    Cabbage Timbale 210
    Calypso Rice with Curried Bananas 202
    Chinese Egg Fried Rice 192
    Mediterranean Rice Salad 52
    Mixed Grain Pilaf 204
    Red Lentil Kedgeree with Avocado & Tomatoes 198

Rice Nuggets in Herby Tomato Sauce 184
Rice-filled Peppers 190
Spanish Baked Tomatoes 68
Spring Vegetable & Herb Risotto 182
Wild Rice Dolmades 188
Rice Nuggets in Herby Tomato Sauce 184
Rice-filled Peppers 190
Rigatoni with Oven-dried Cherry Tomatoes & Mascarpone 148
Roasted Aubergine Dip with Pitta Strips 76
Roasted Butternut Squash 94
Roasted Mixed Vegetables with Garlic & Herb Sauce 92
Roasted Red Pepper, Tomato & Red Onion Soup 106
Roasted Vegetable Pie 166

S
Savoury Wontons 72
Spaghettini with Lemon Pesto & Cheese & Herb Bread 138
Spaghettini with Peas, Spring Onions & Mint 144
Spanish Baked Tomatoes 68
Spiced Couscous & Vegetables 46
Spinach & Ricotta Gnocchi with Butter & Italian Hard Cheese 142
Spinach Dhal 240
Spinach Dumplings with Rich Tomato Sauce 220
Spinach, Pine Nut & Mascarpone Pizza 172
Spring Vegetable & Herb Risotto 182

Stilton, Tomato & Courgette Quiche 160
Stuffed Onions with Pine Nuts 70
Swede, Turnip, Parsnip & Potato Soup 104
Sweet Potato Cakes with Mango & Tomato Salsa 82
Sweetcorn Fritters 74

T
Tagliarini with Broad Beans, Saffron & Crème Fraîche 152
Tagliatelle with Broccoli & Sesame 130
Thai Noodles & Vegetables with Tofu 252
Thai Stuffed Eggs with Spinach & Sesame Seeds 88
Tomato & Basil Soup 112
Tomato & Courgette Herb Tart 168
Tortellini & Summer Vegetable Salad 54

V
Vegetable & Coconut Stew 120
Vegetable Frittata 224
Vegetable Kofta Curry 236
Vegetables Braised in Olive Oil & Lemon 98
Vegetables in Coconut Milk with Rice Noodles 250
Vegetarian Cassoulet 216
Vegetarian Spaghetti Bolognese 128

W
Warm Noodle Salad with Sesame & Peanut Dressing 60
Wild Rice Dolmades 188
Winter Coleslaw 44